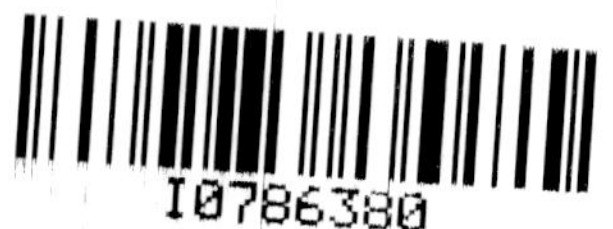

HEDGEROW

COLORING BOOK

MIDNIGHT EDITION

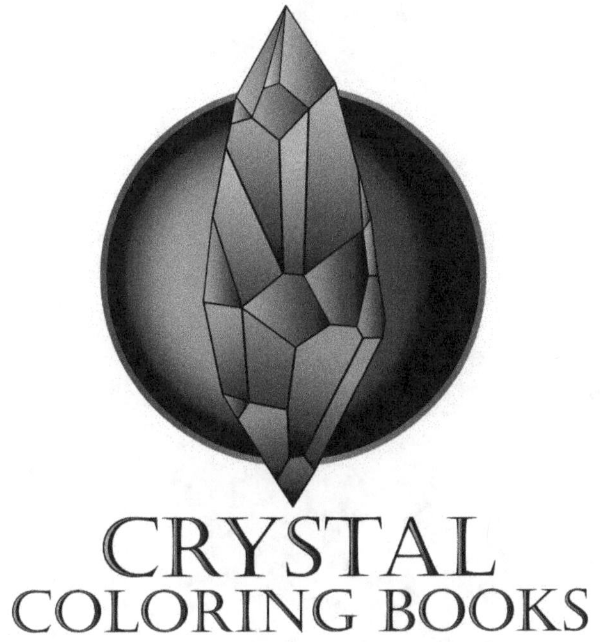

ISBN-13: 978-1725879225
ISBN-10: 1725879220

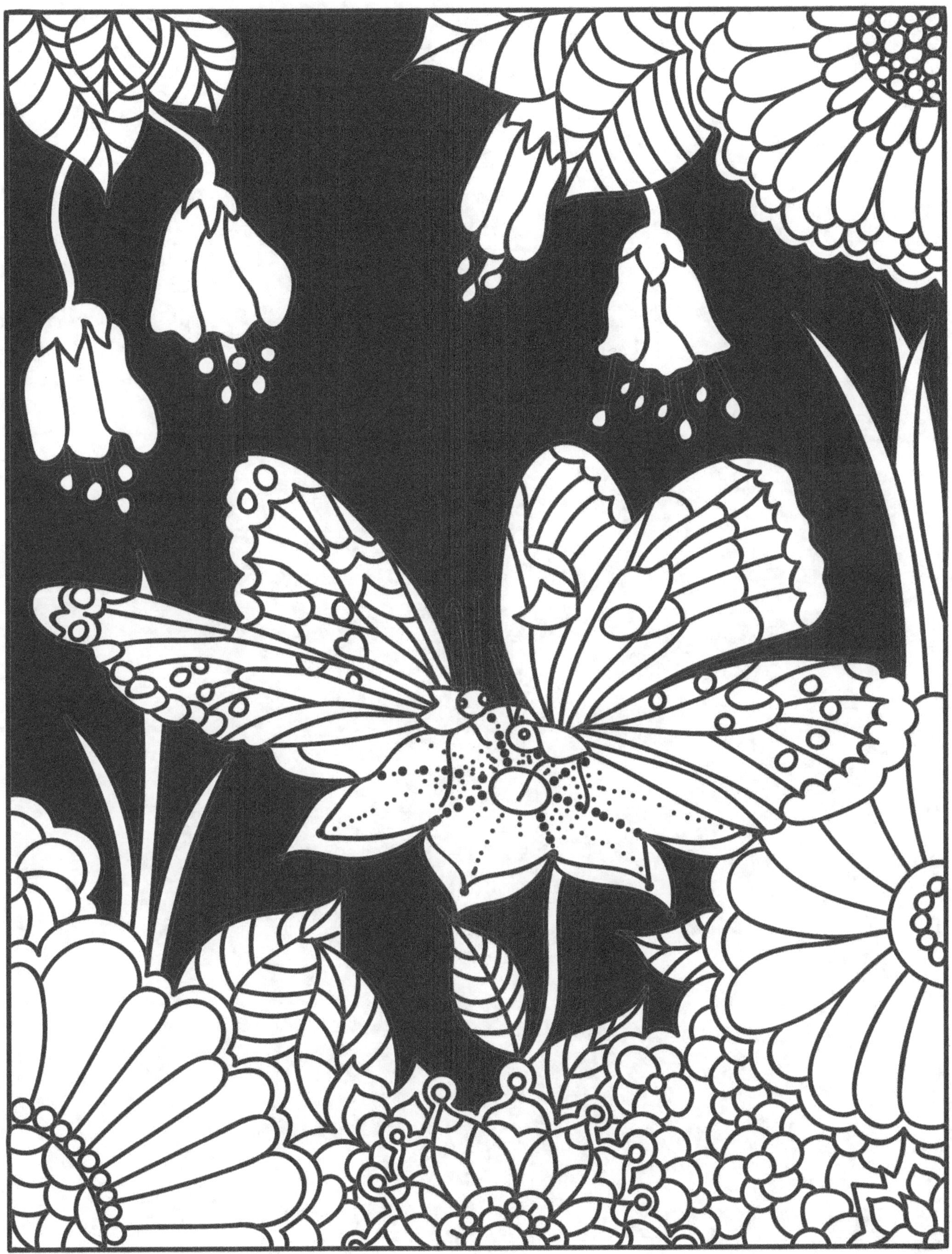

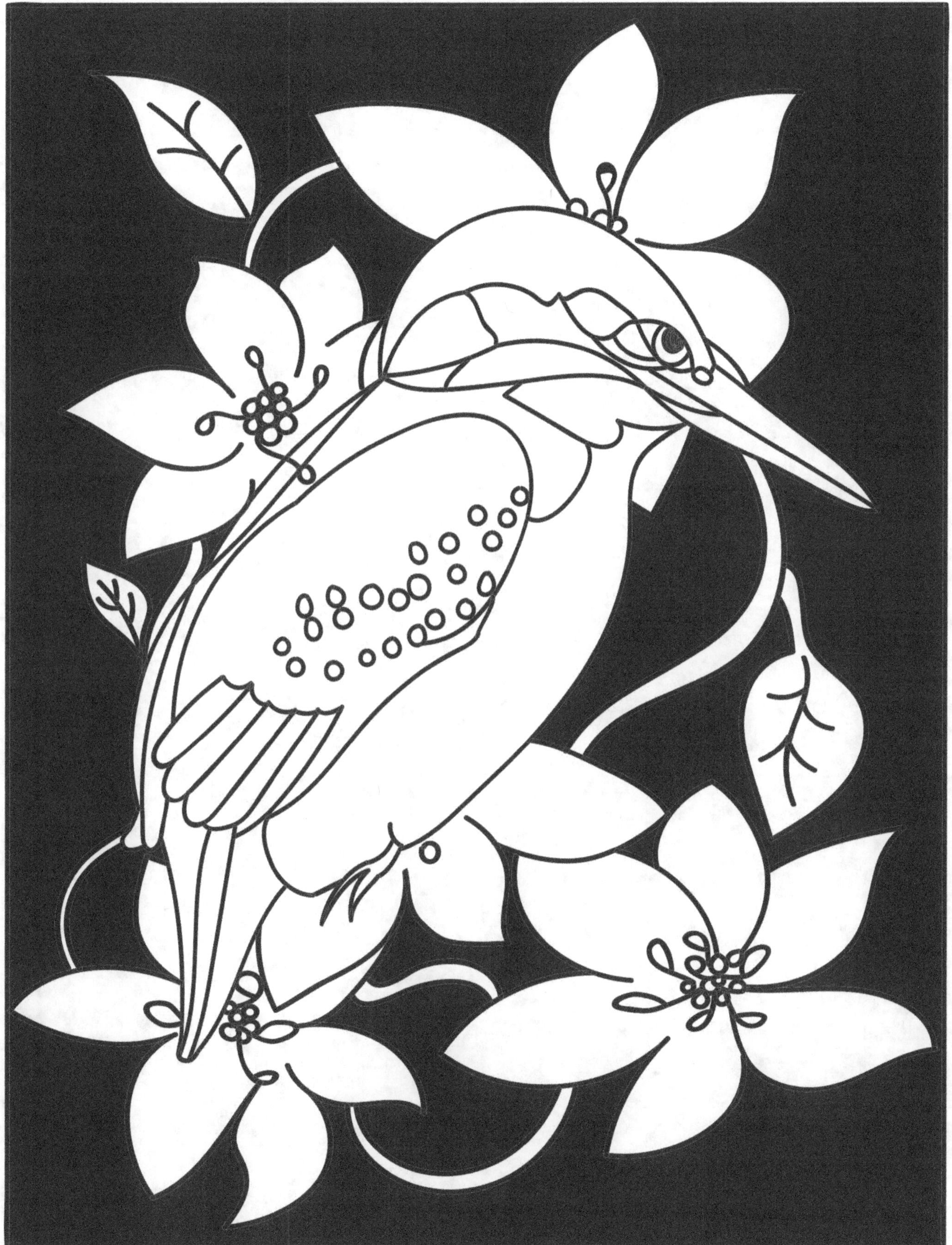

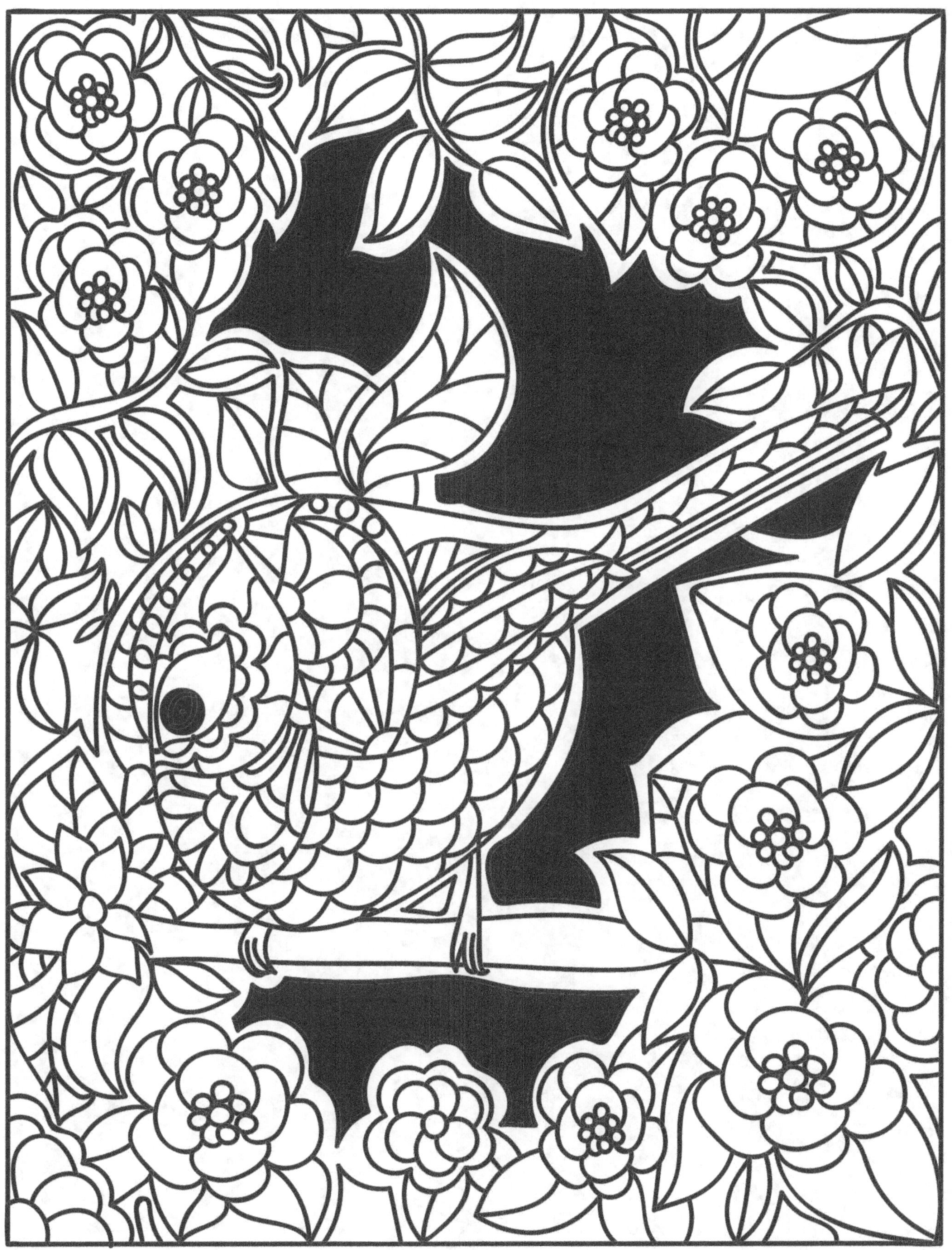

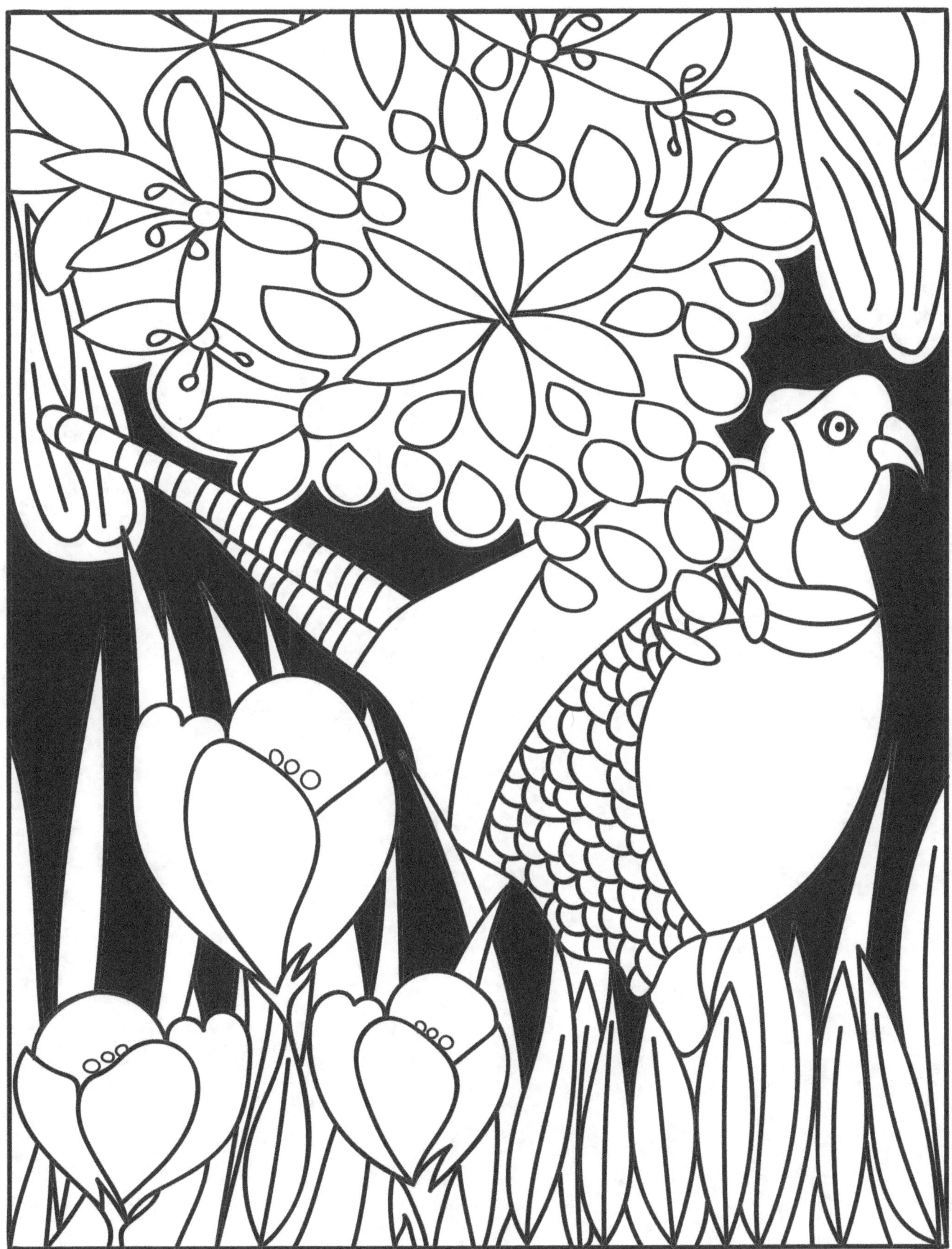

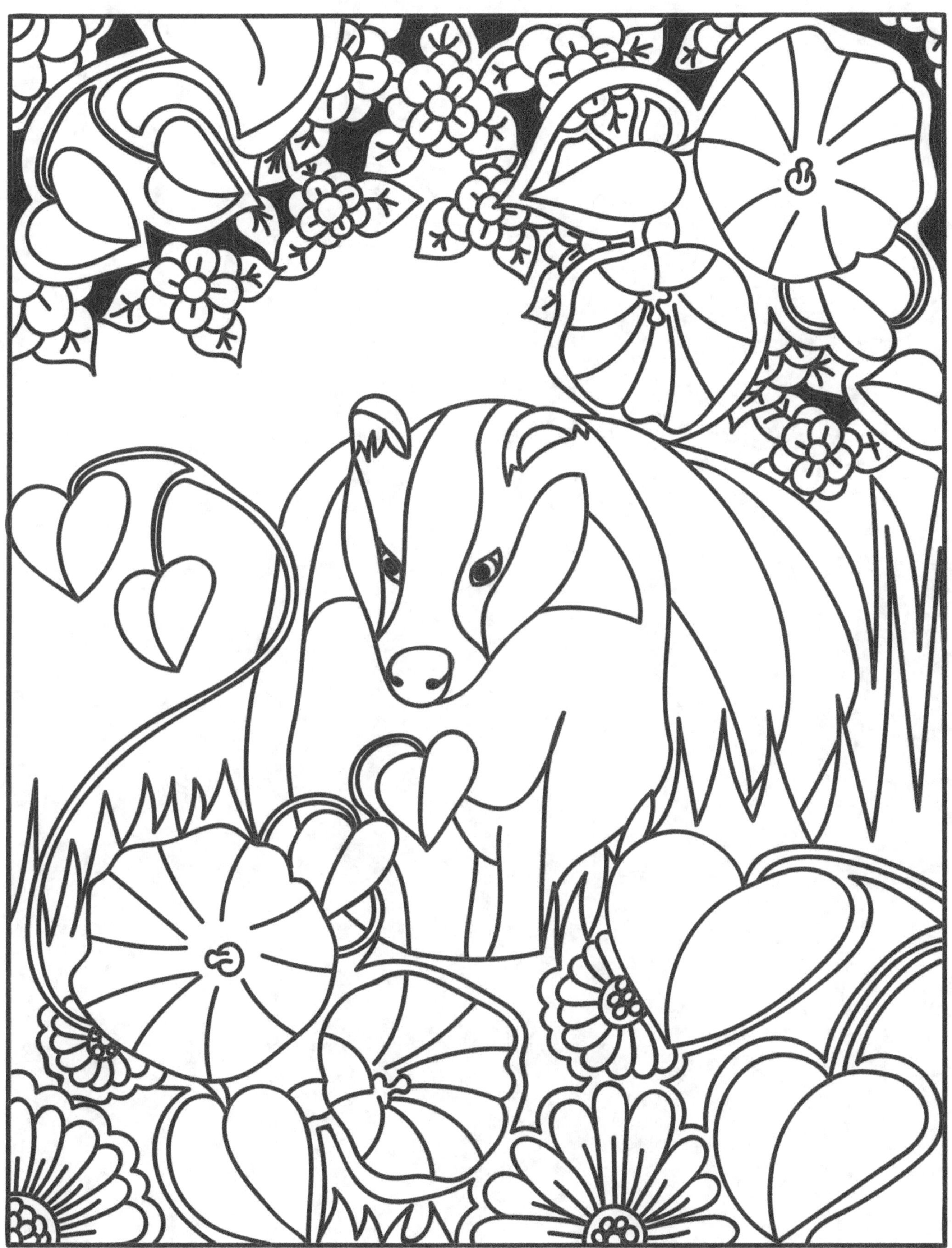

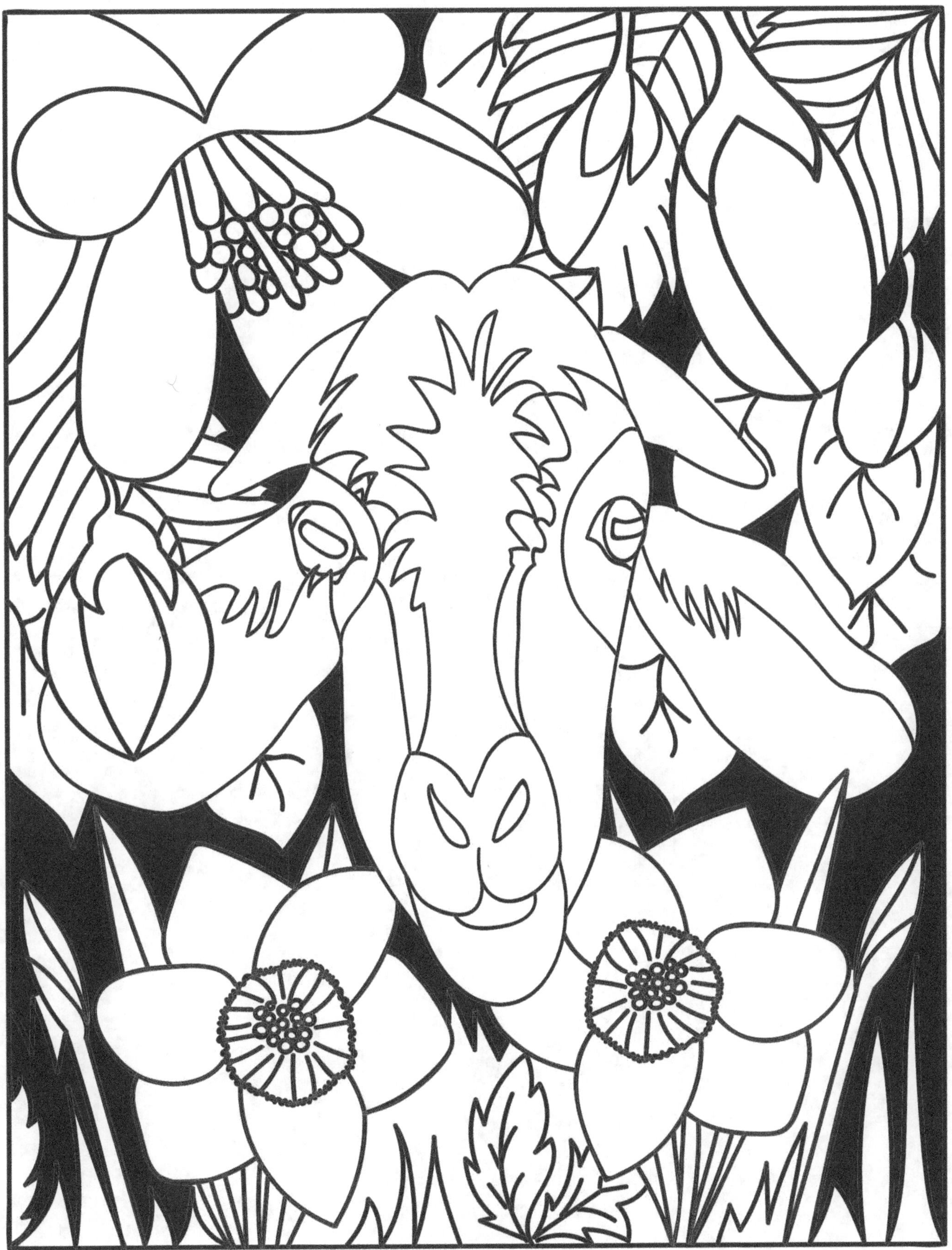

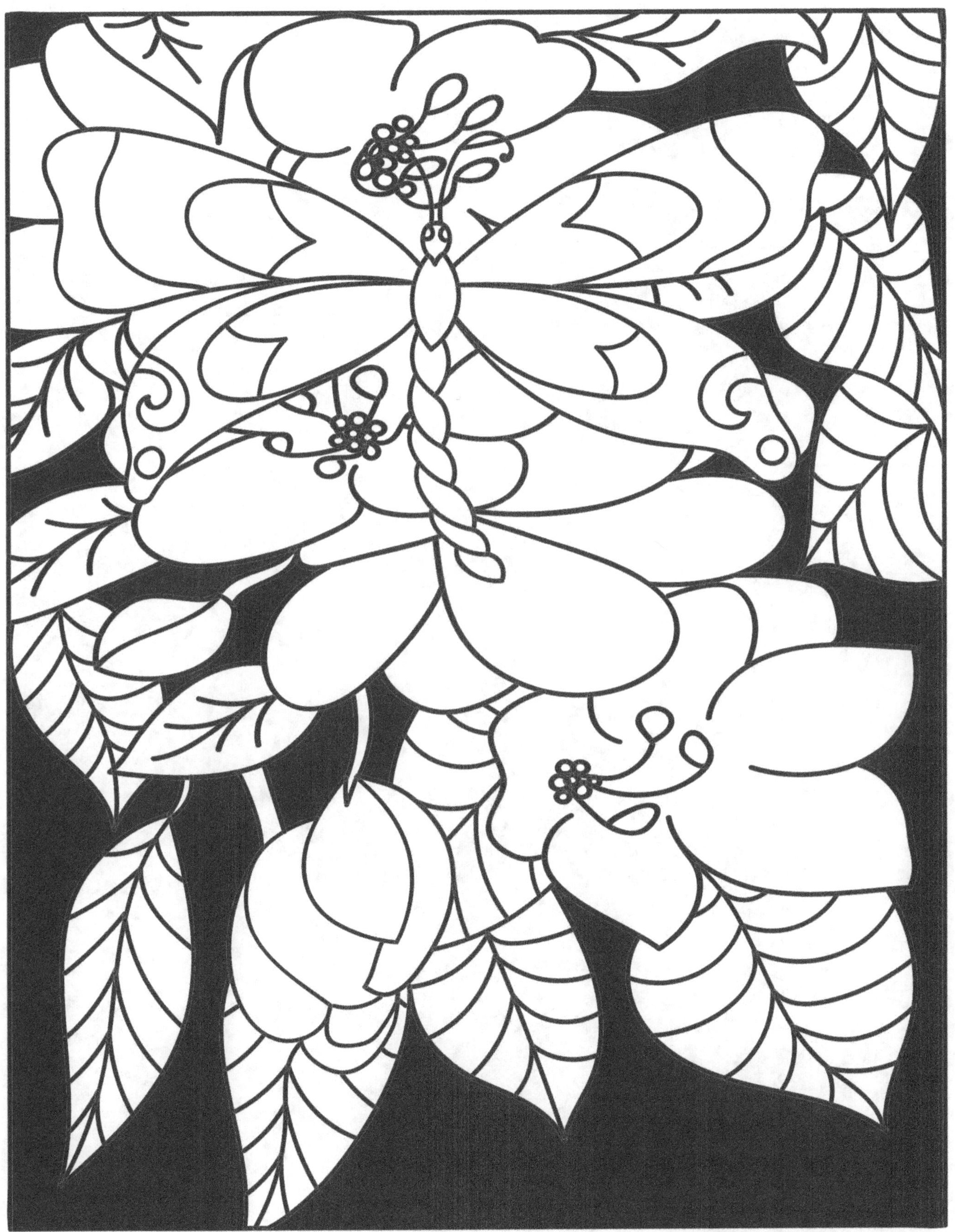

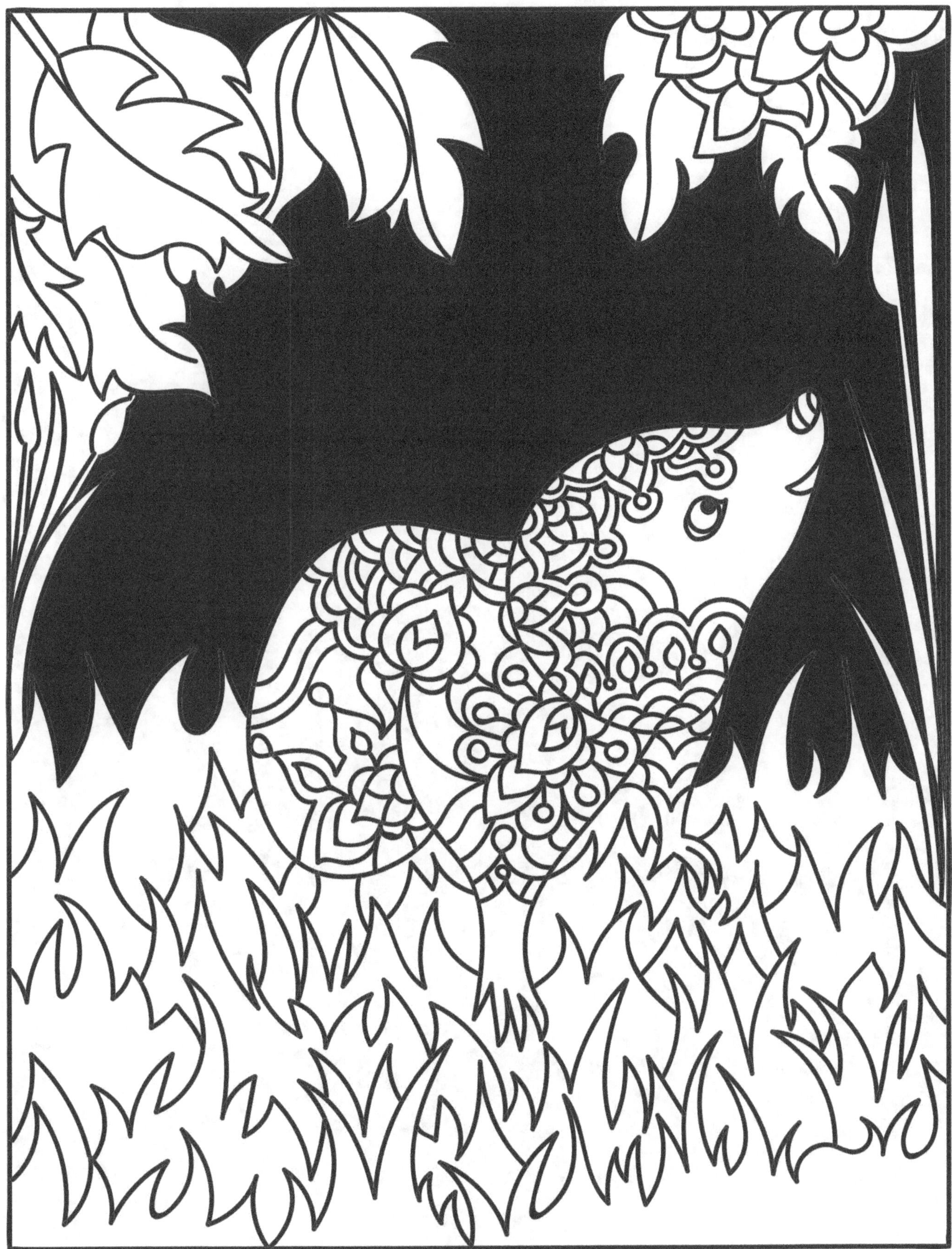

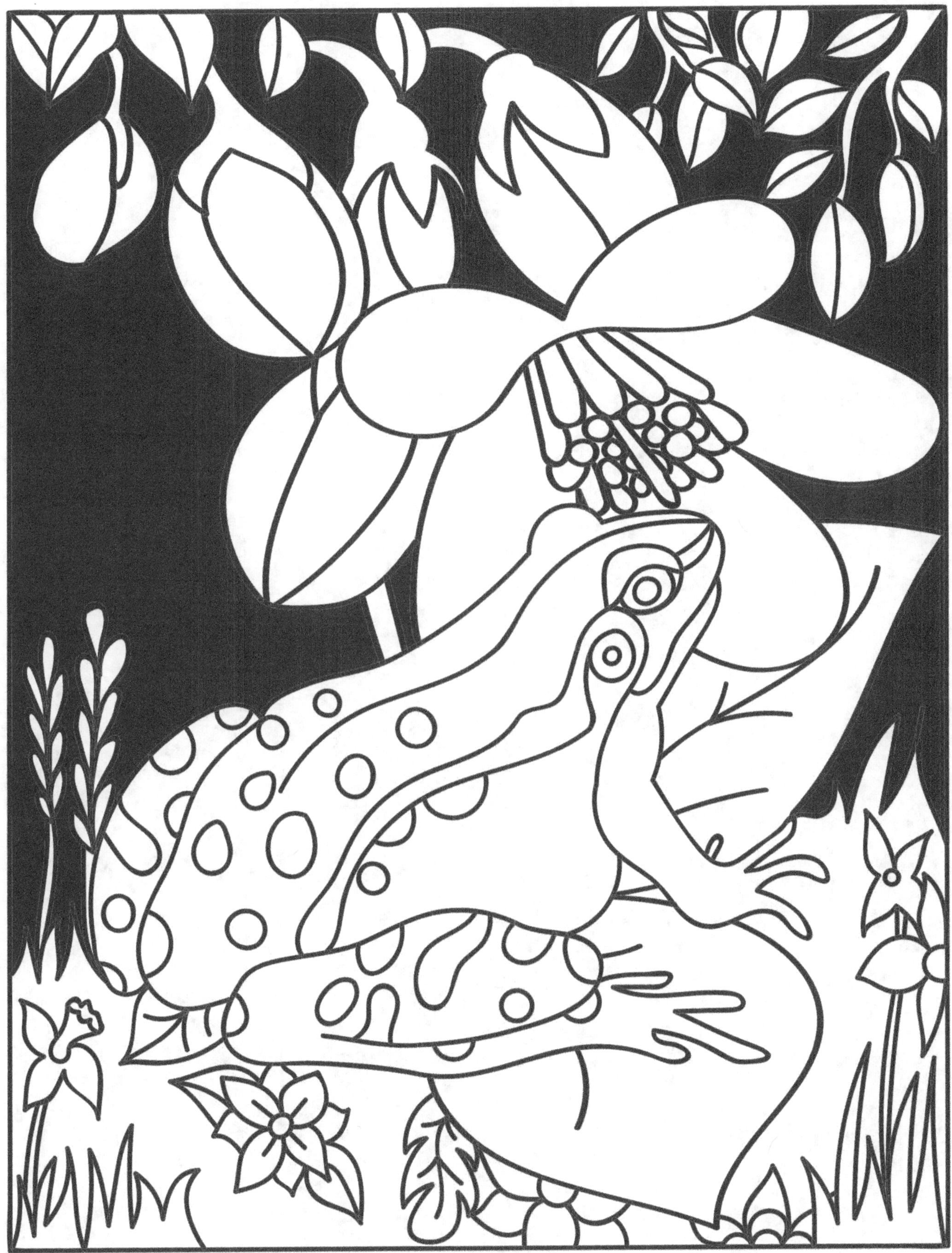

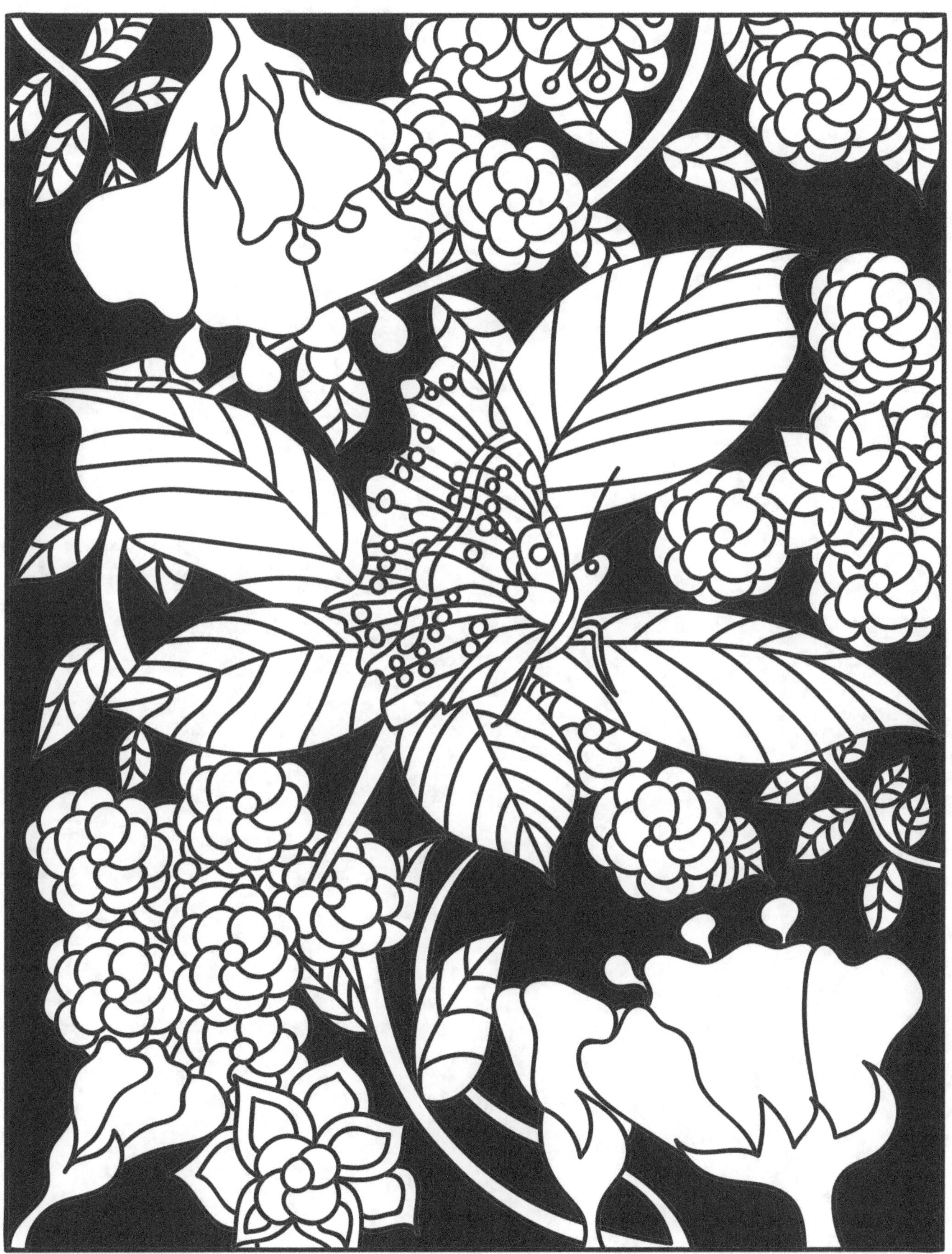

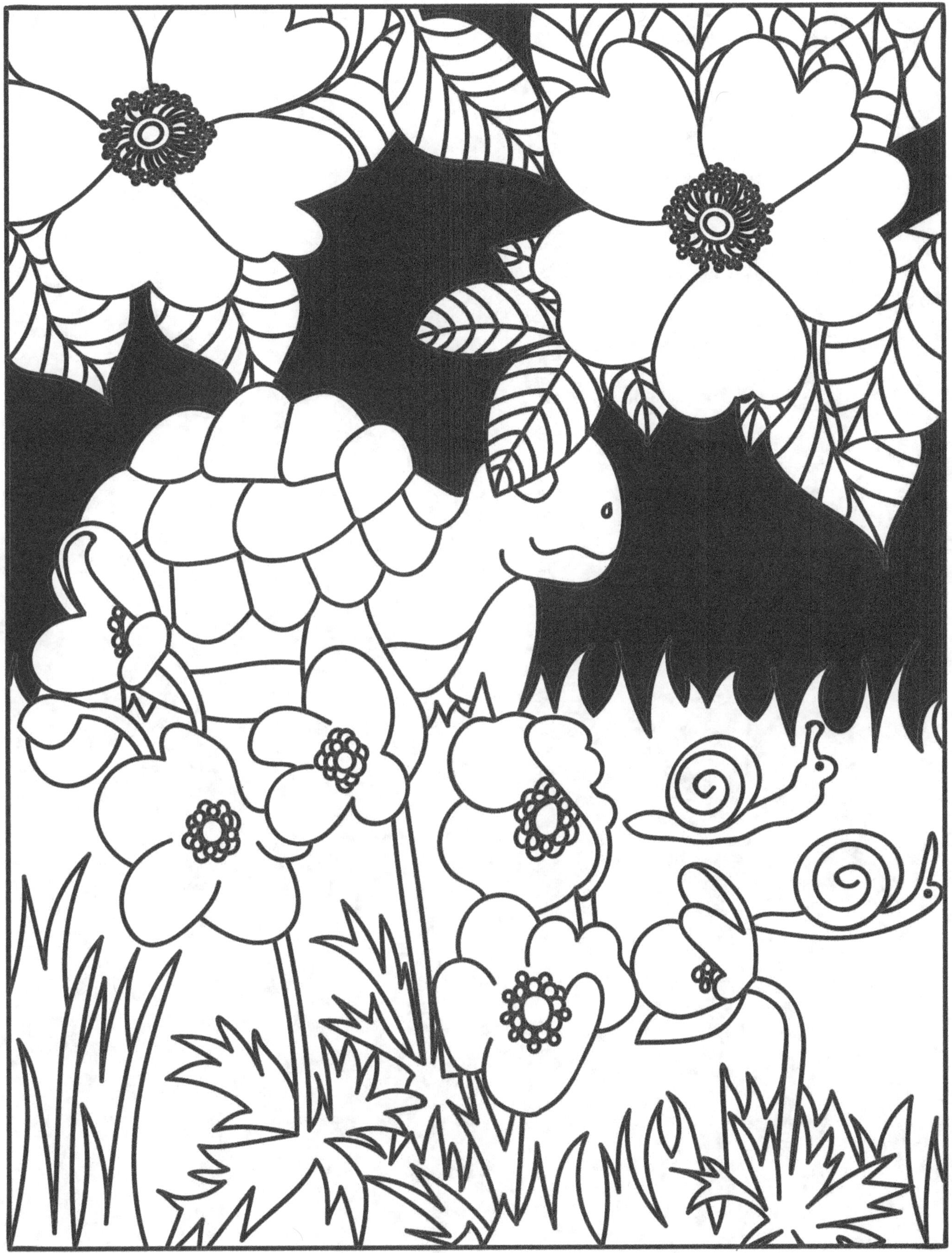

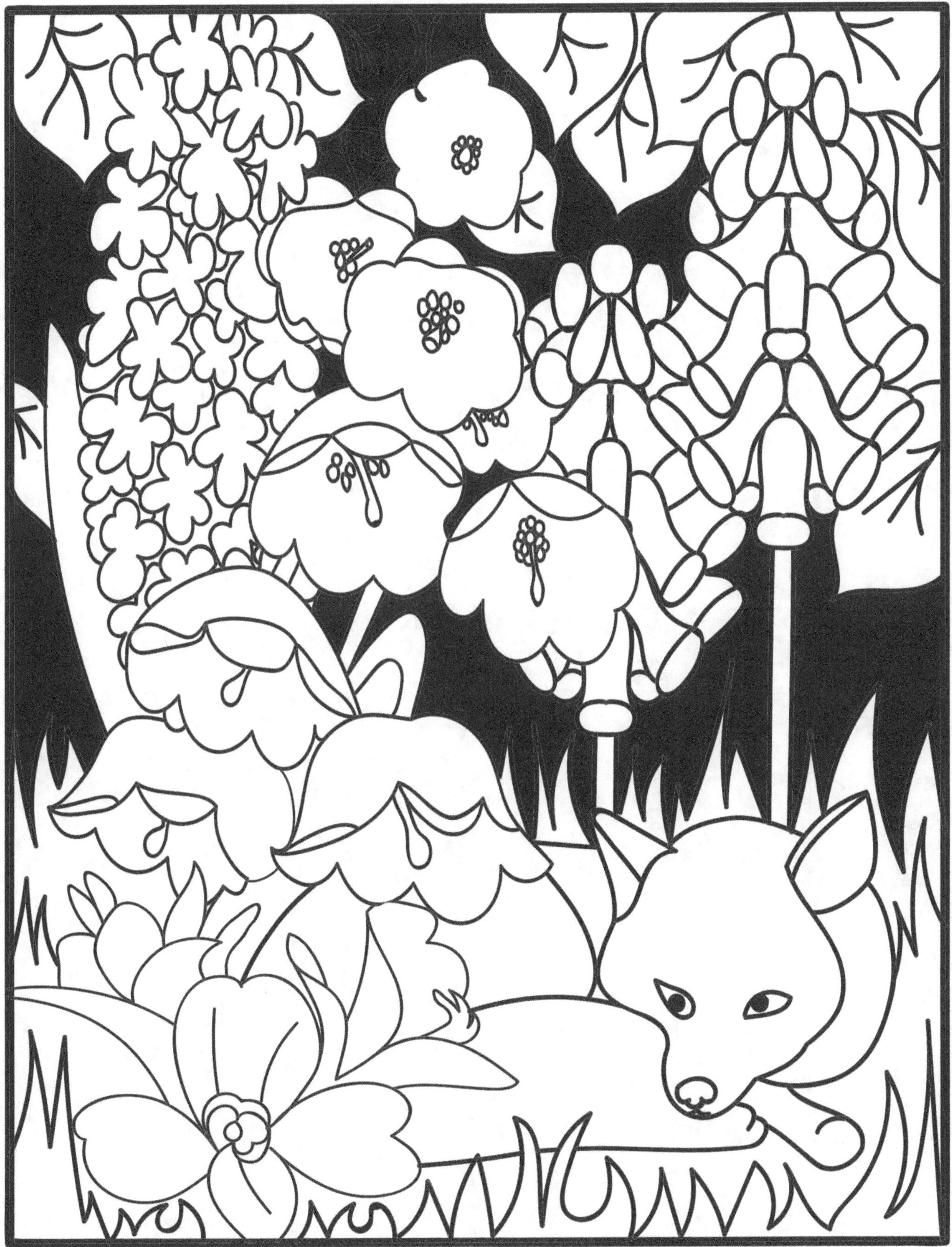

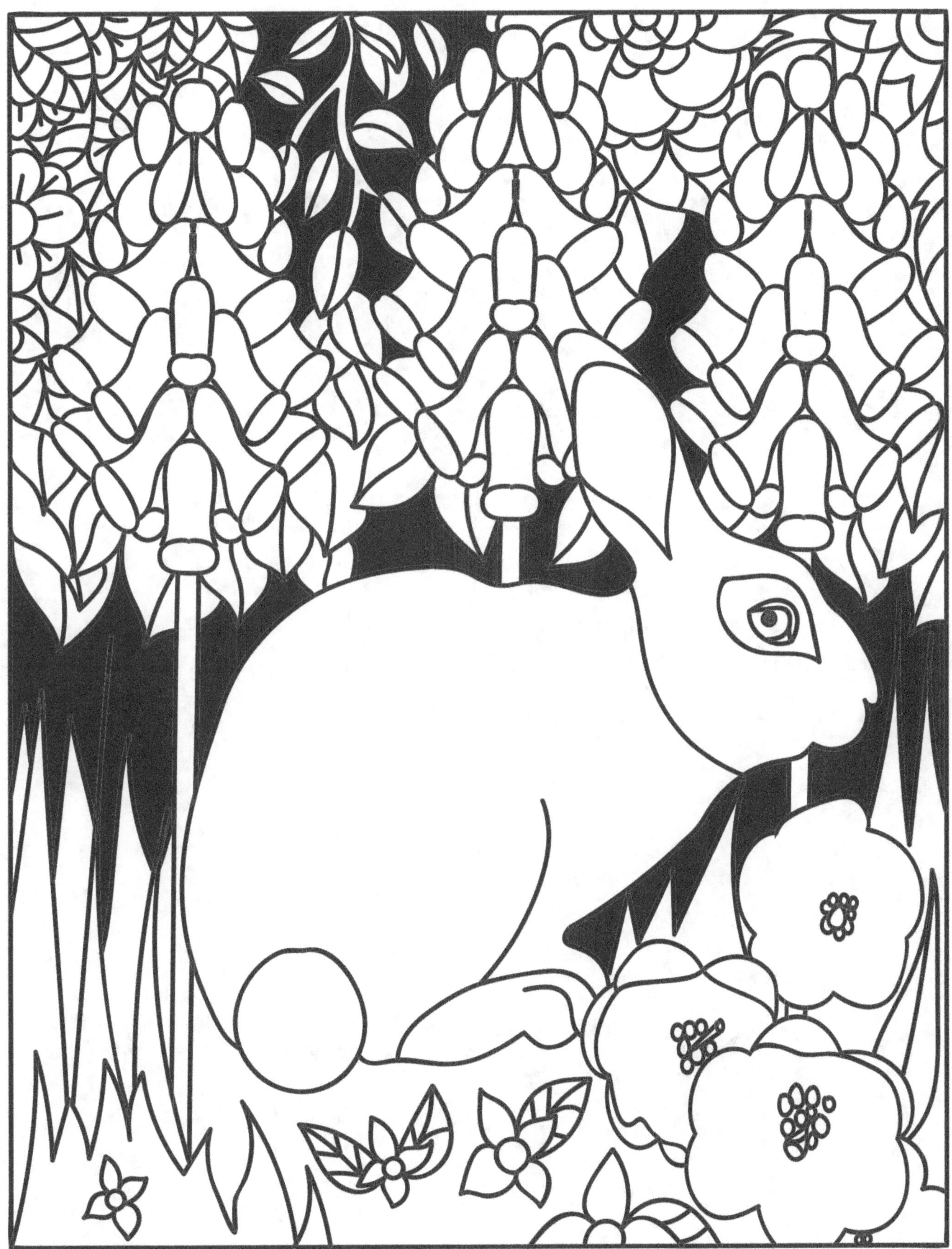

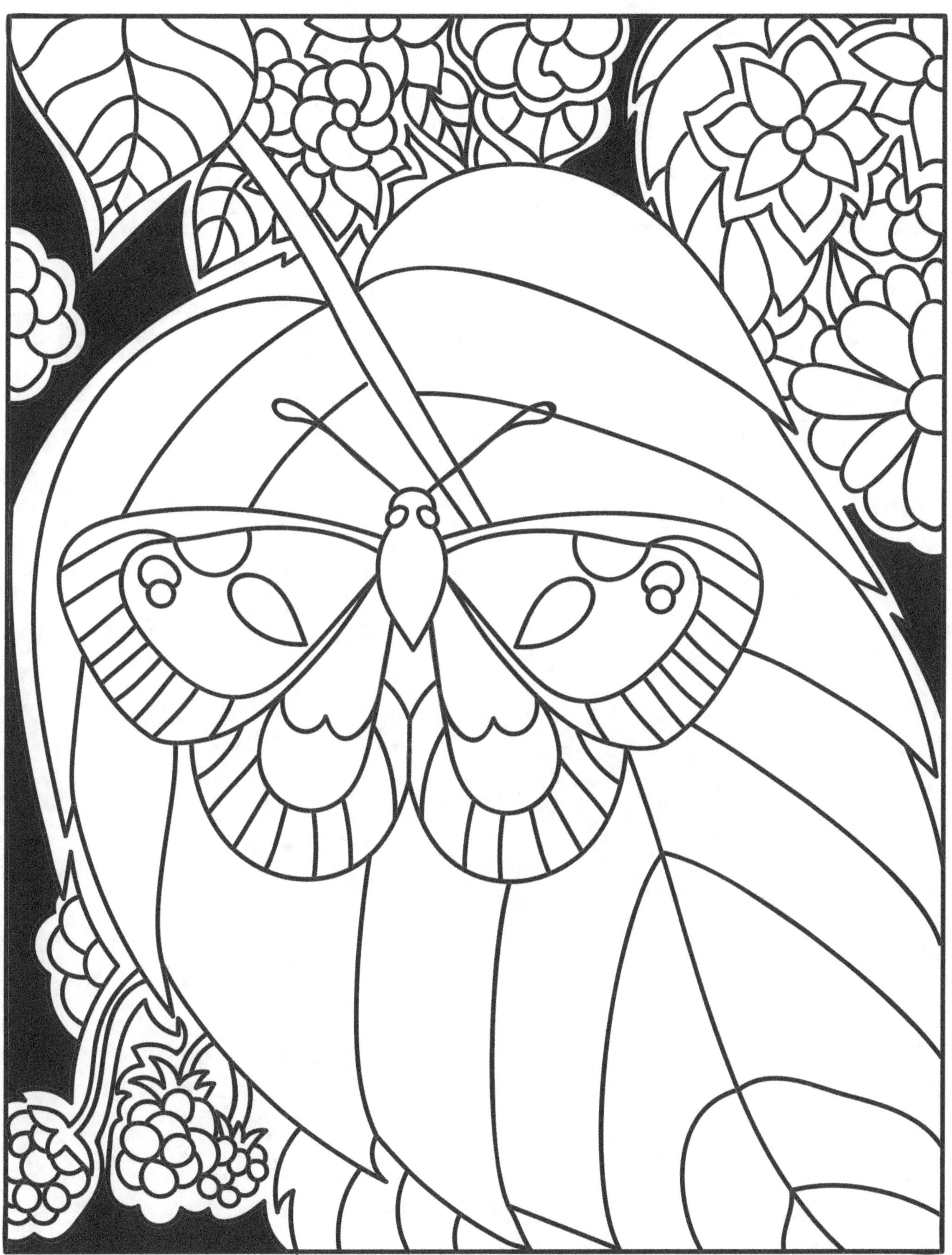

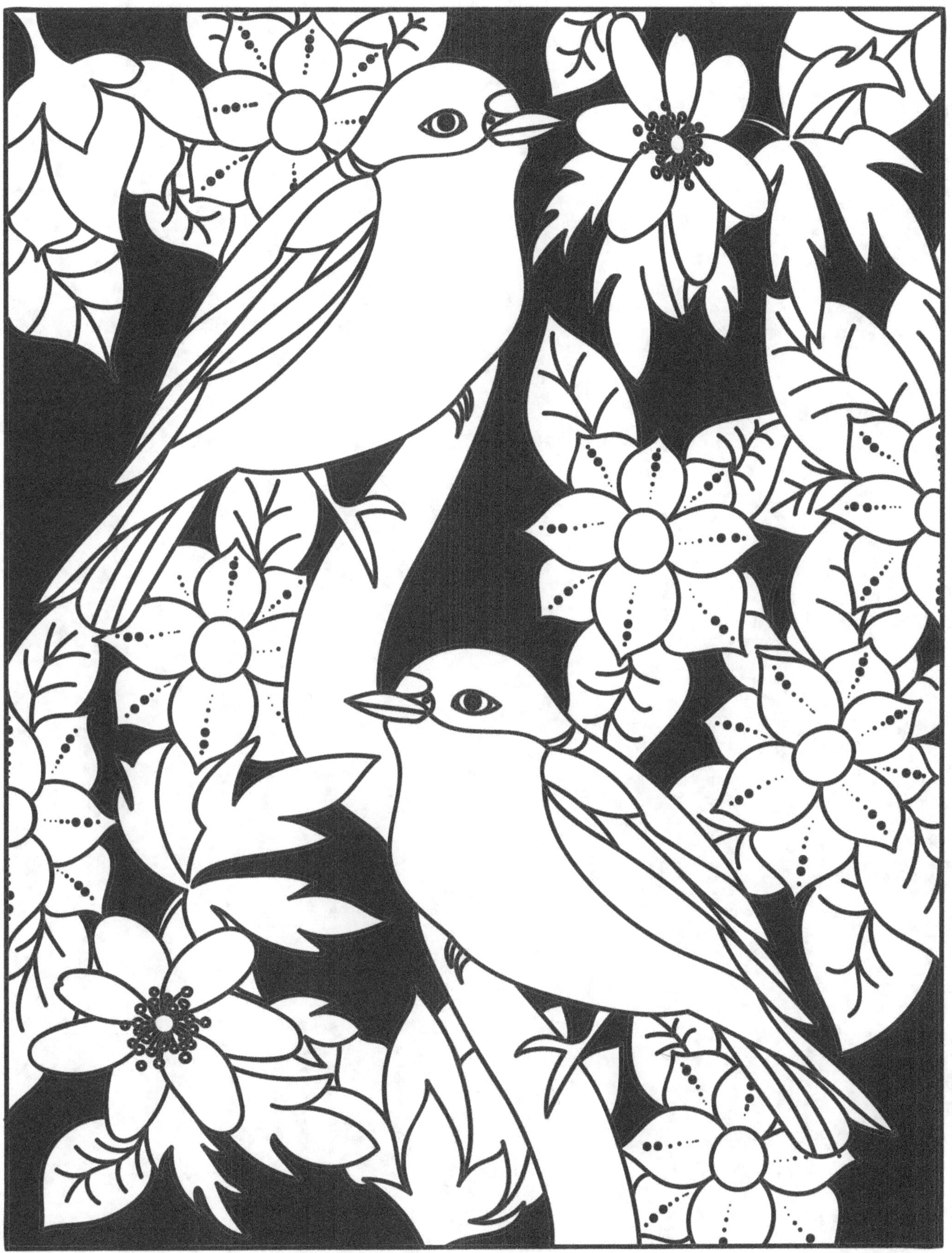

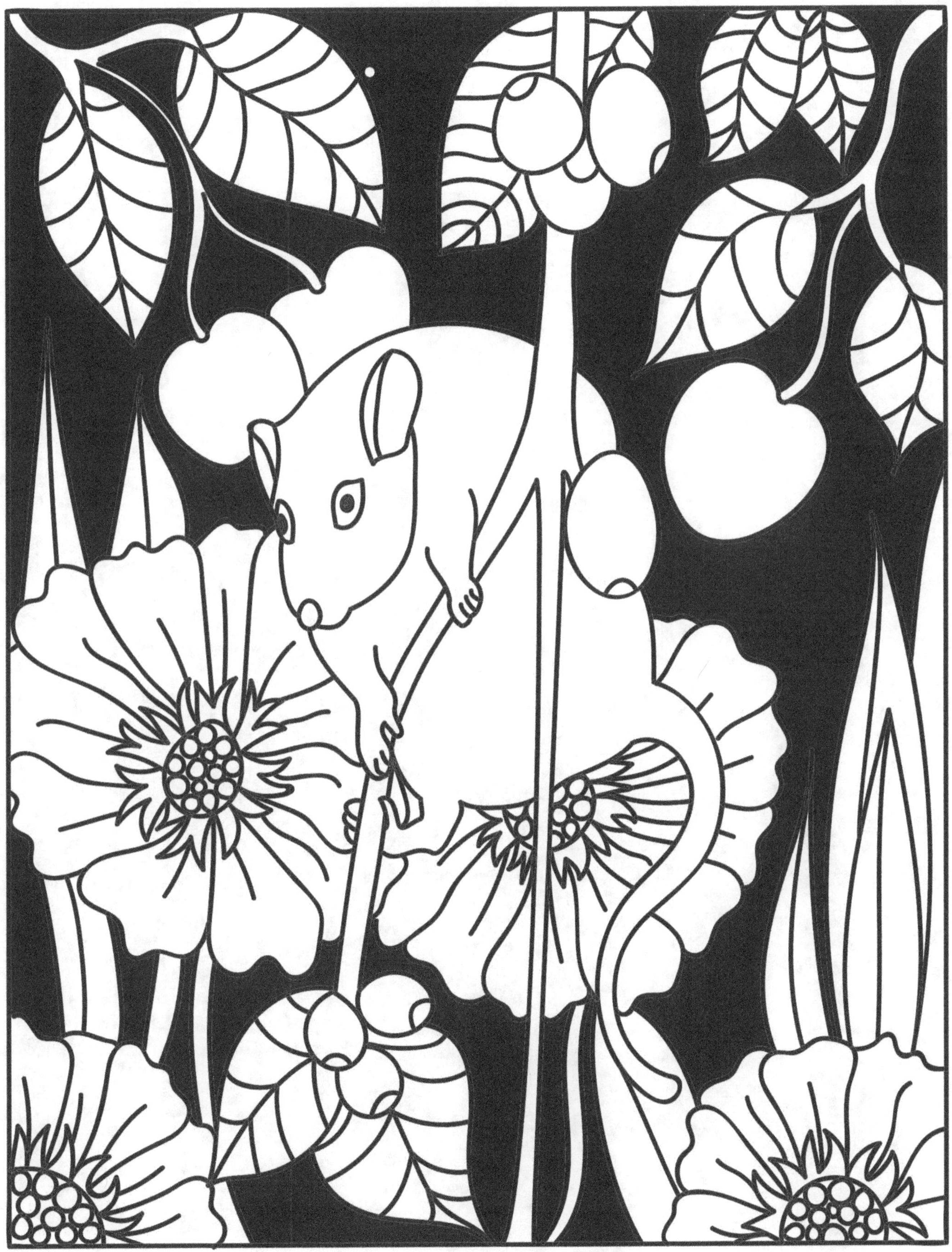

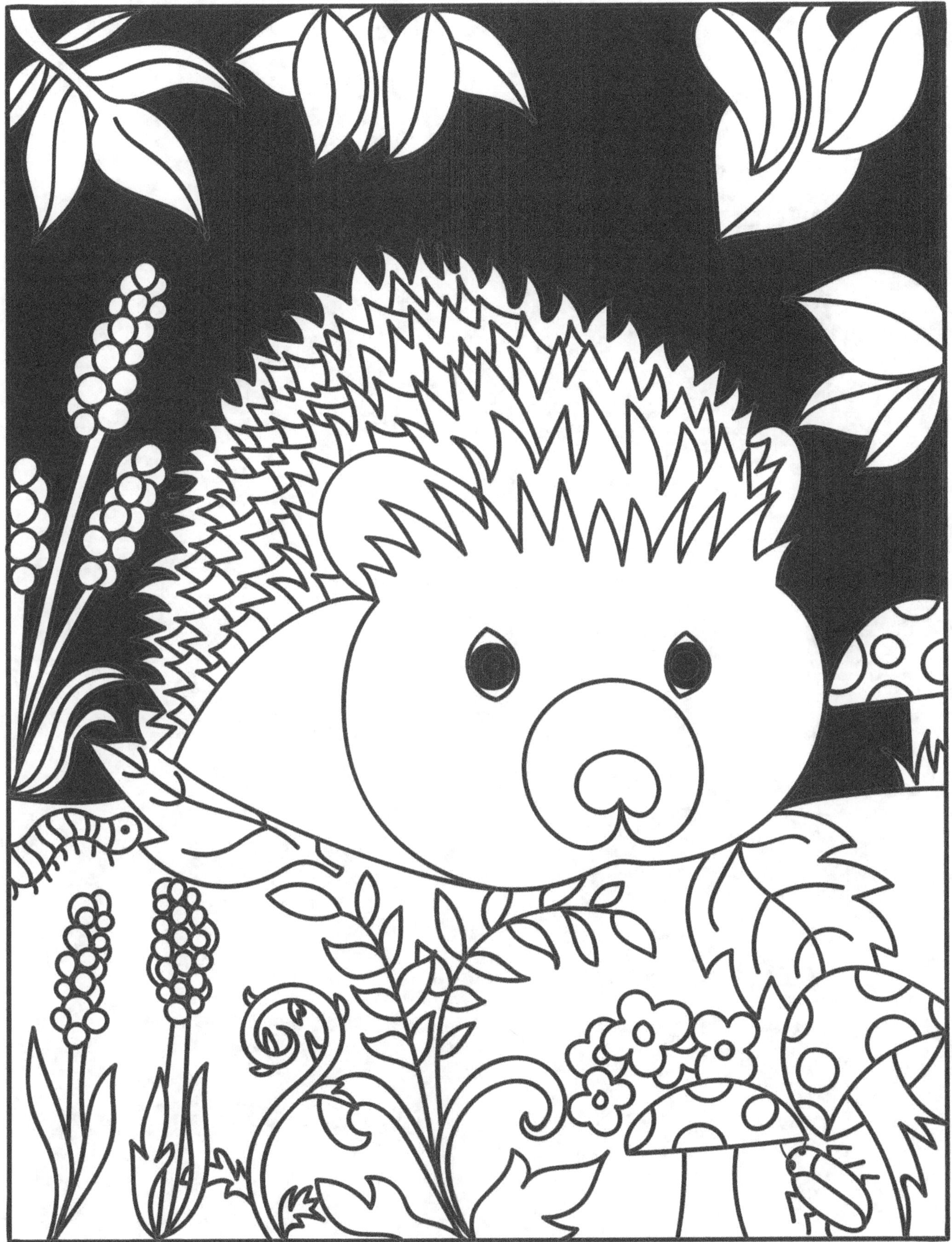

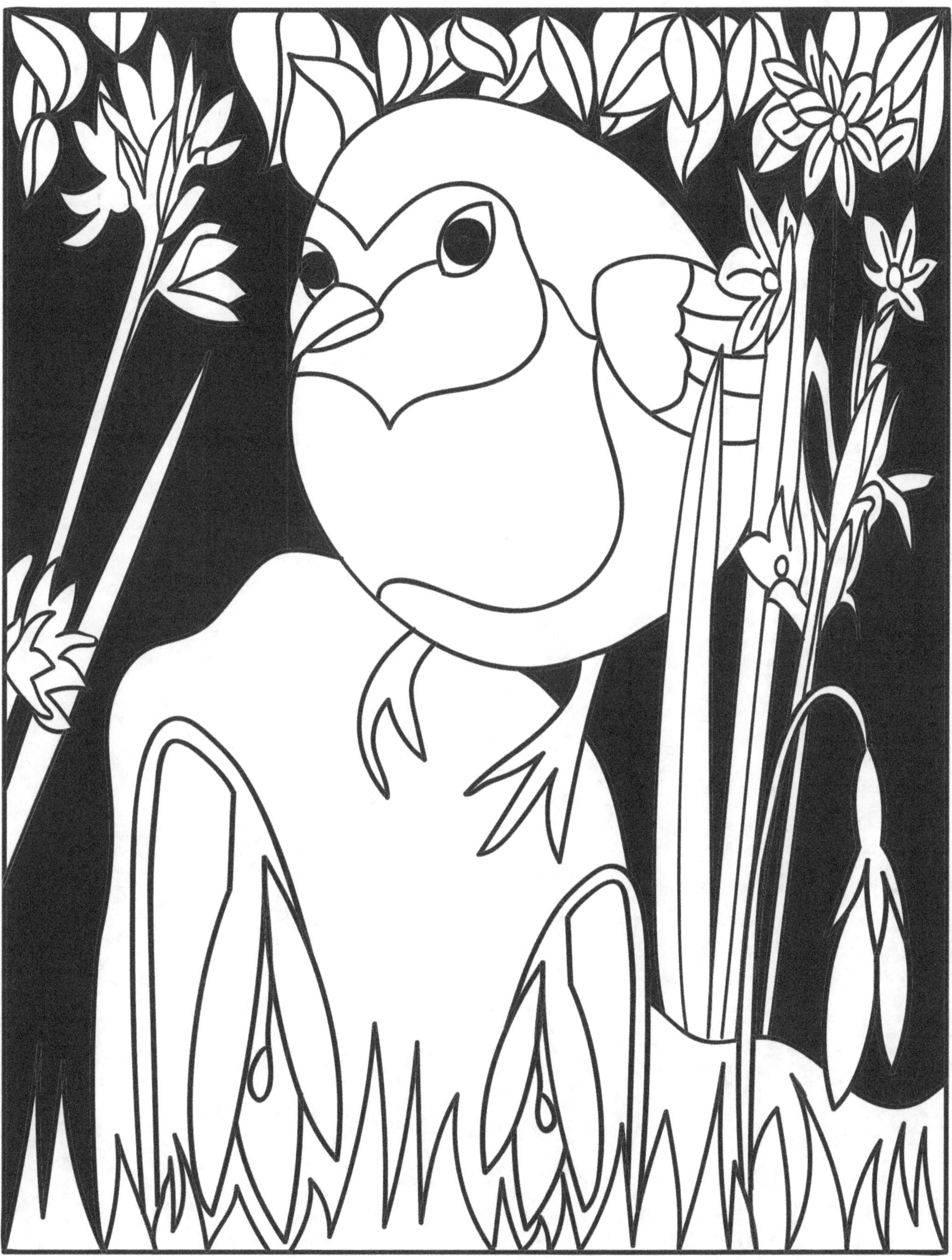

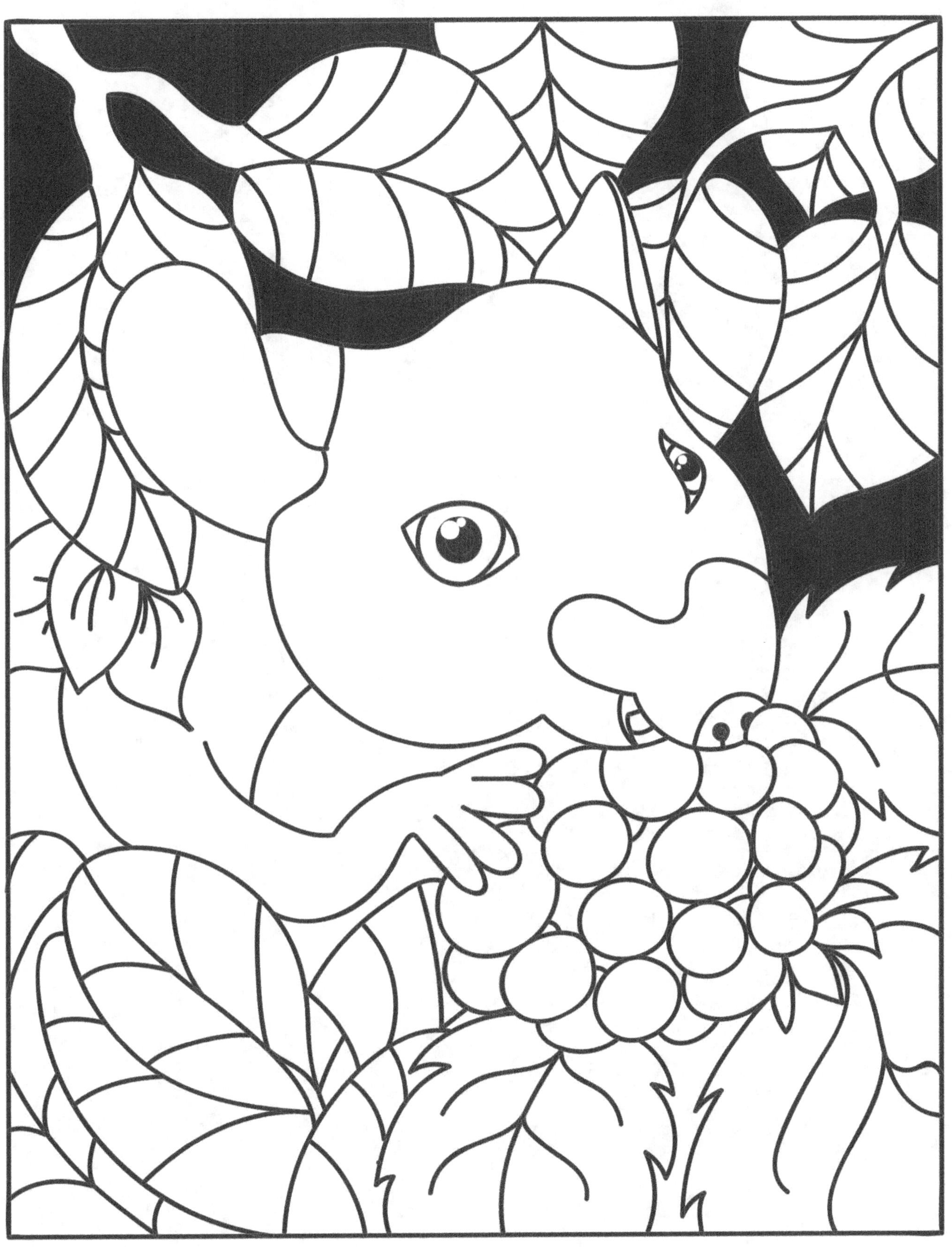

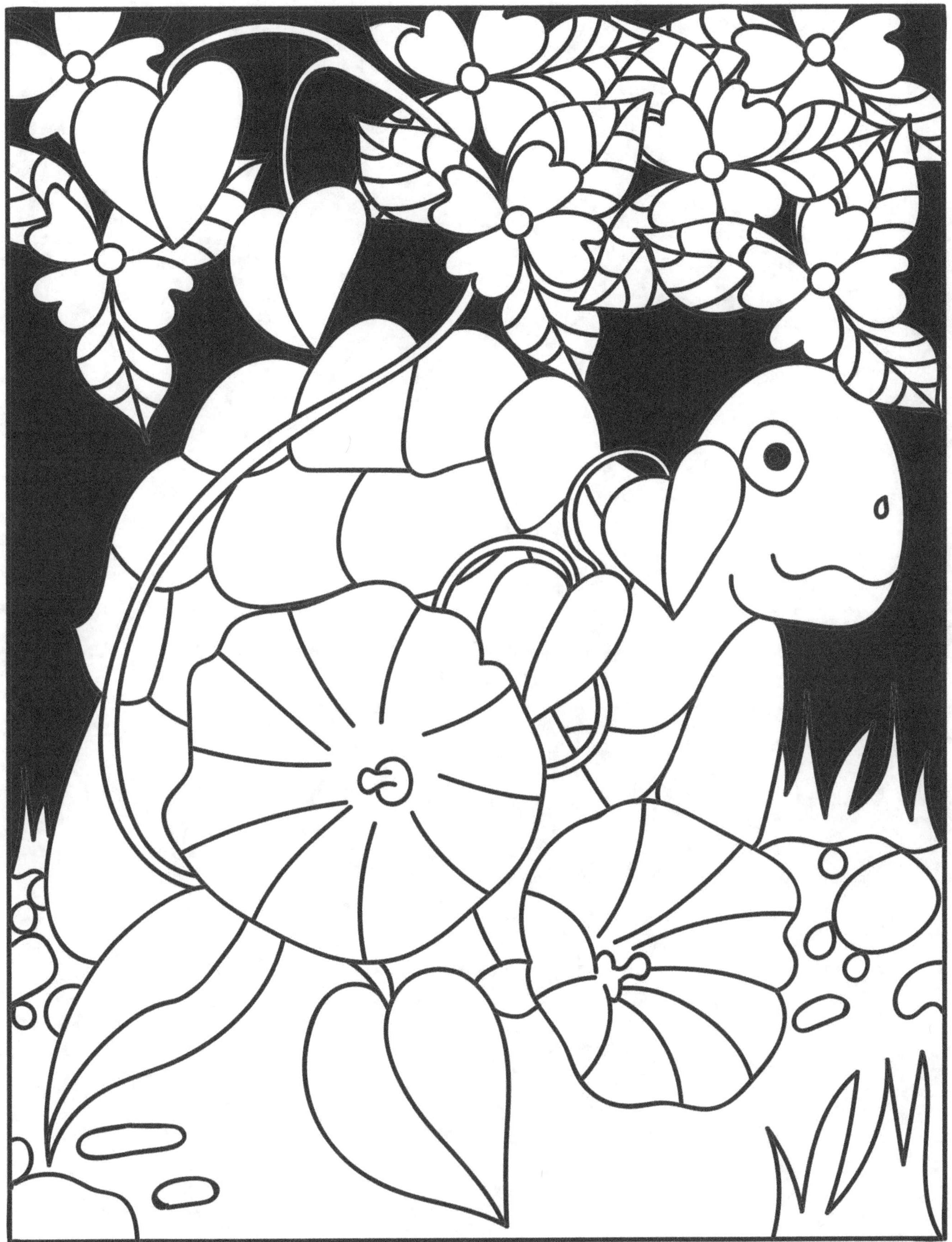

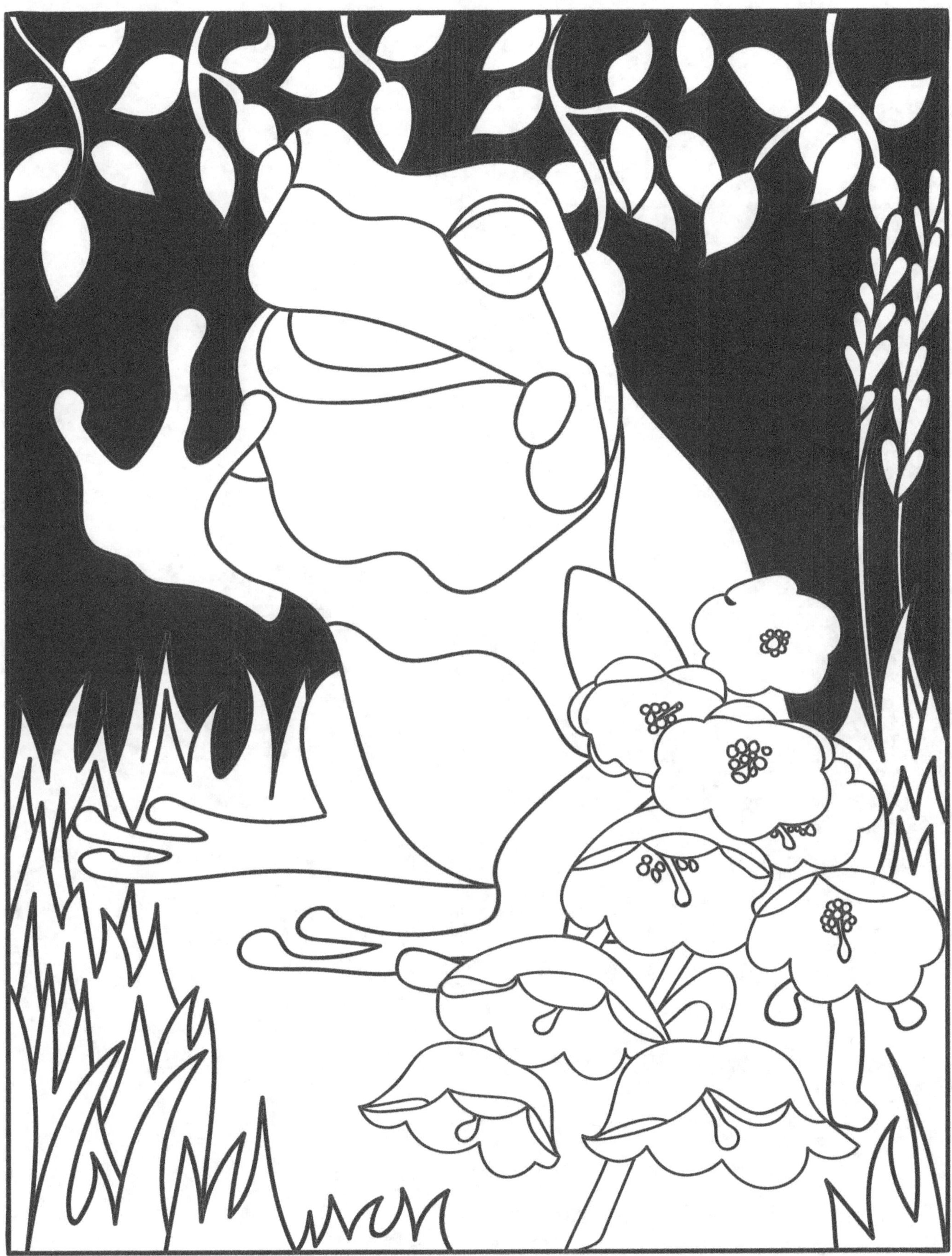

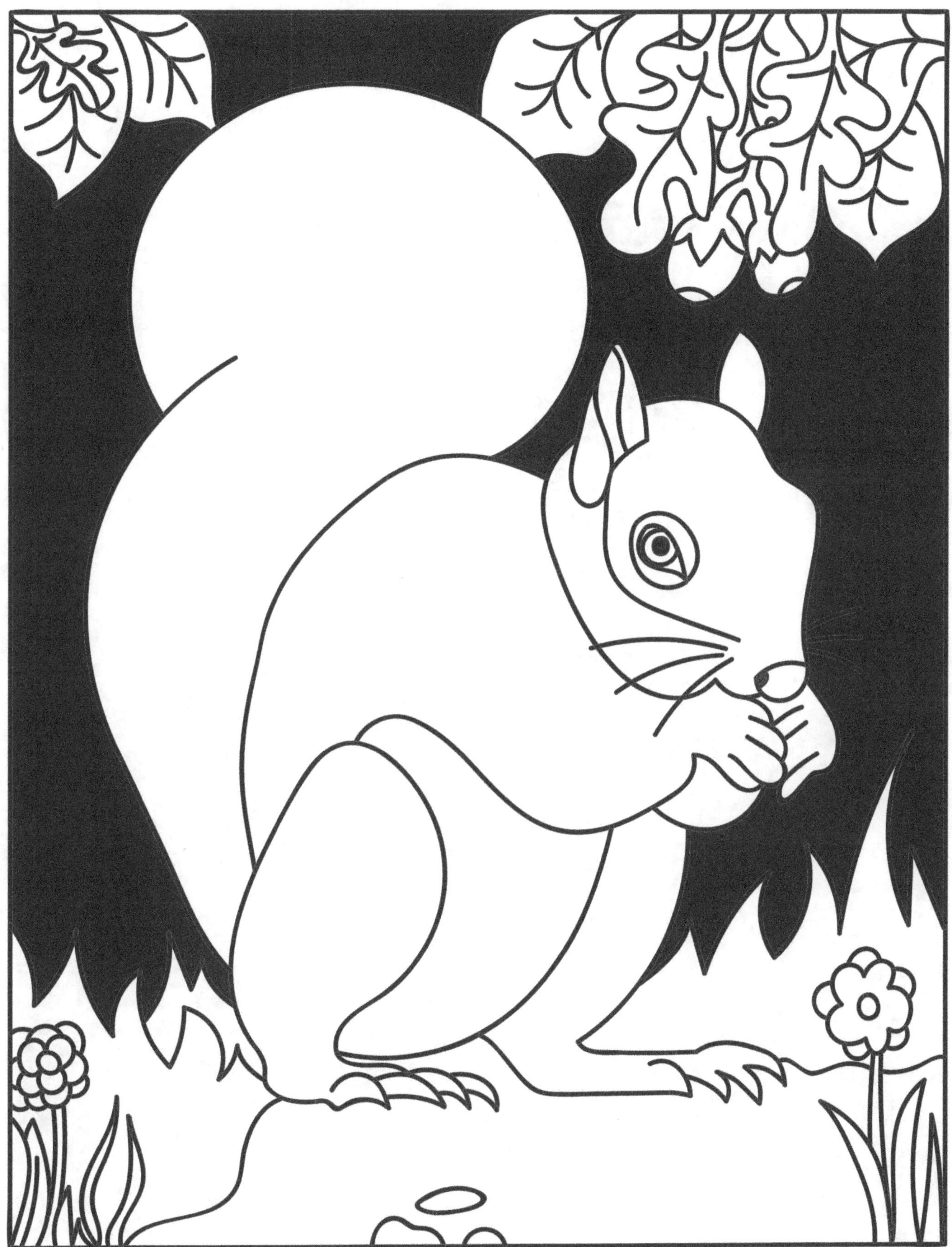

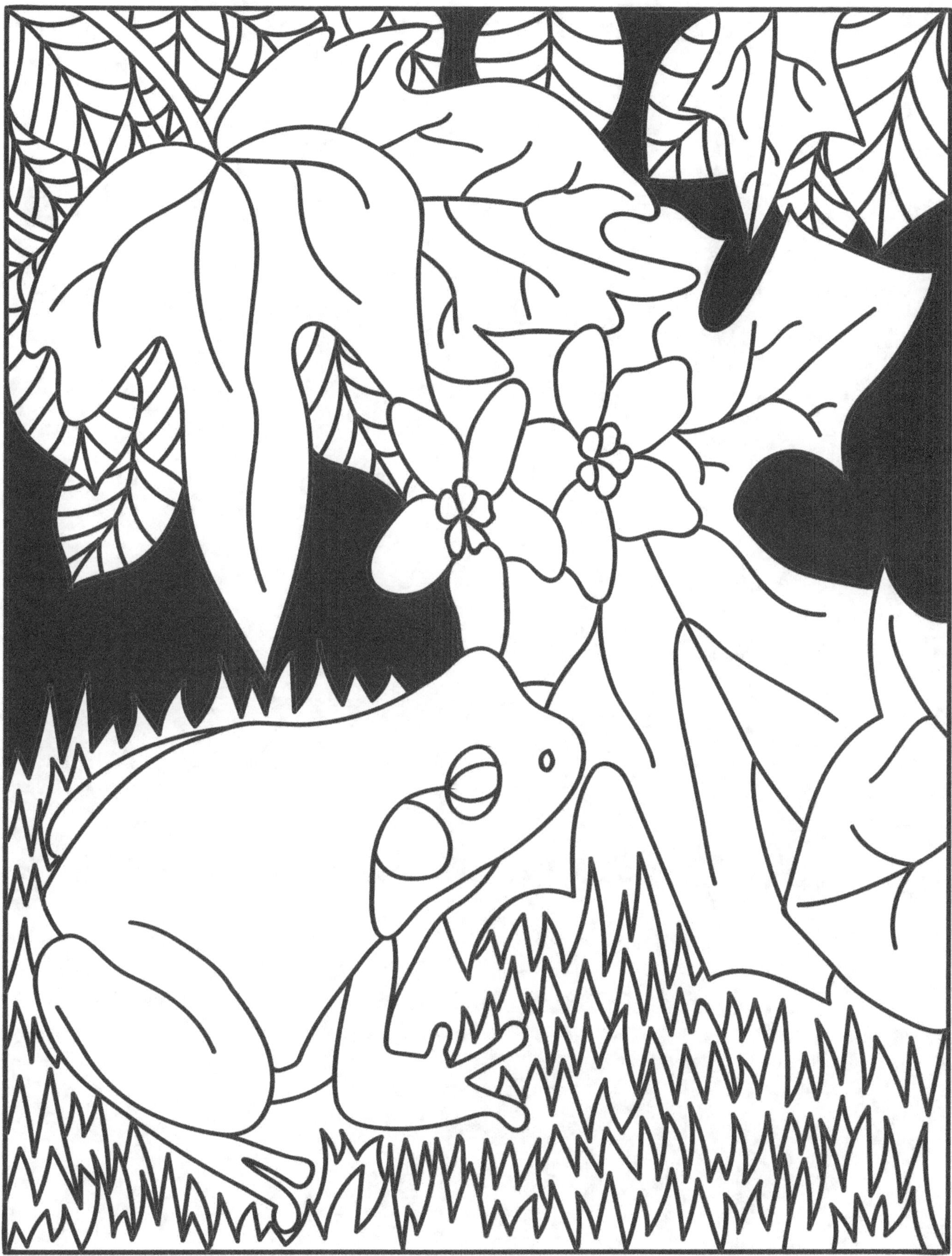

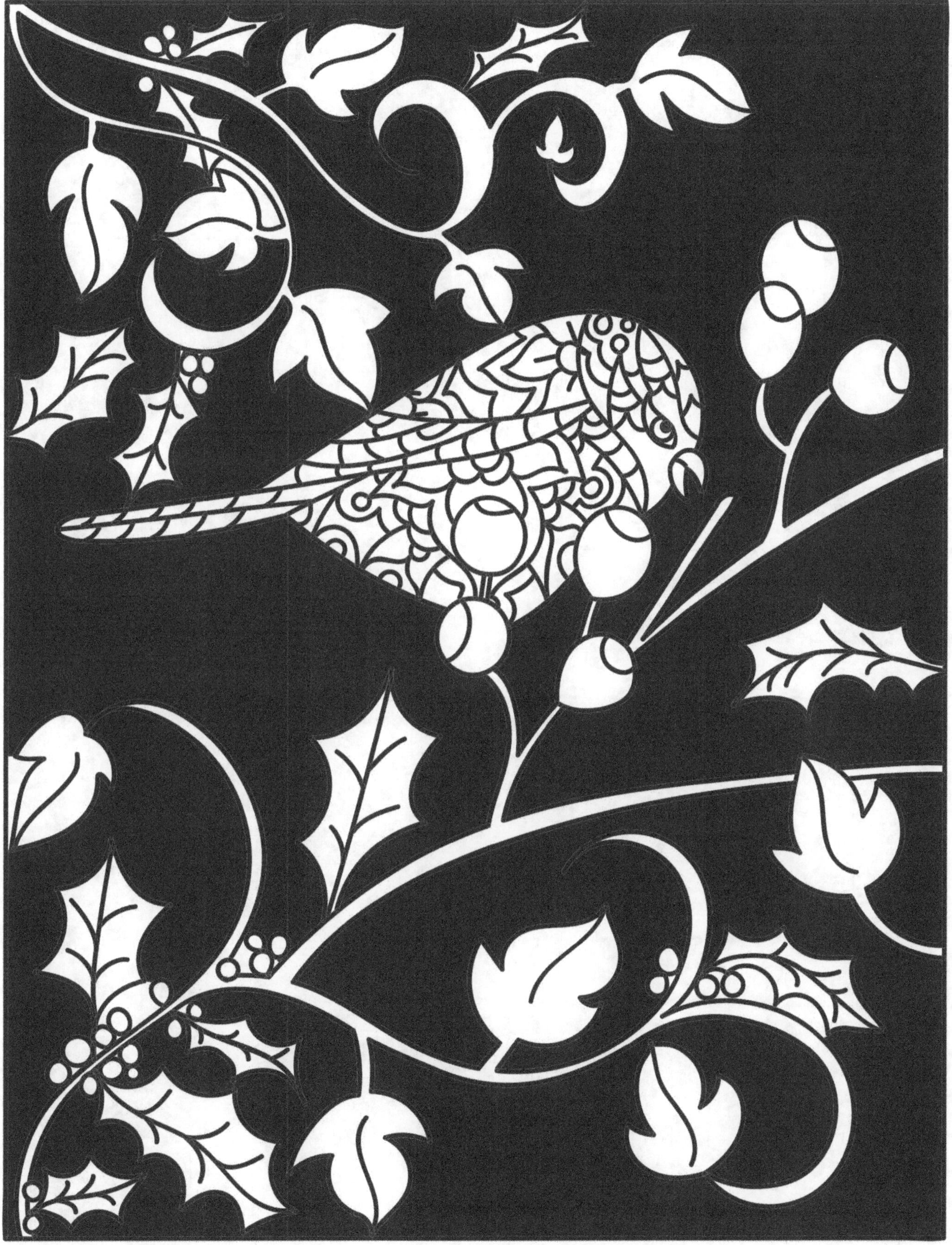

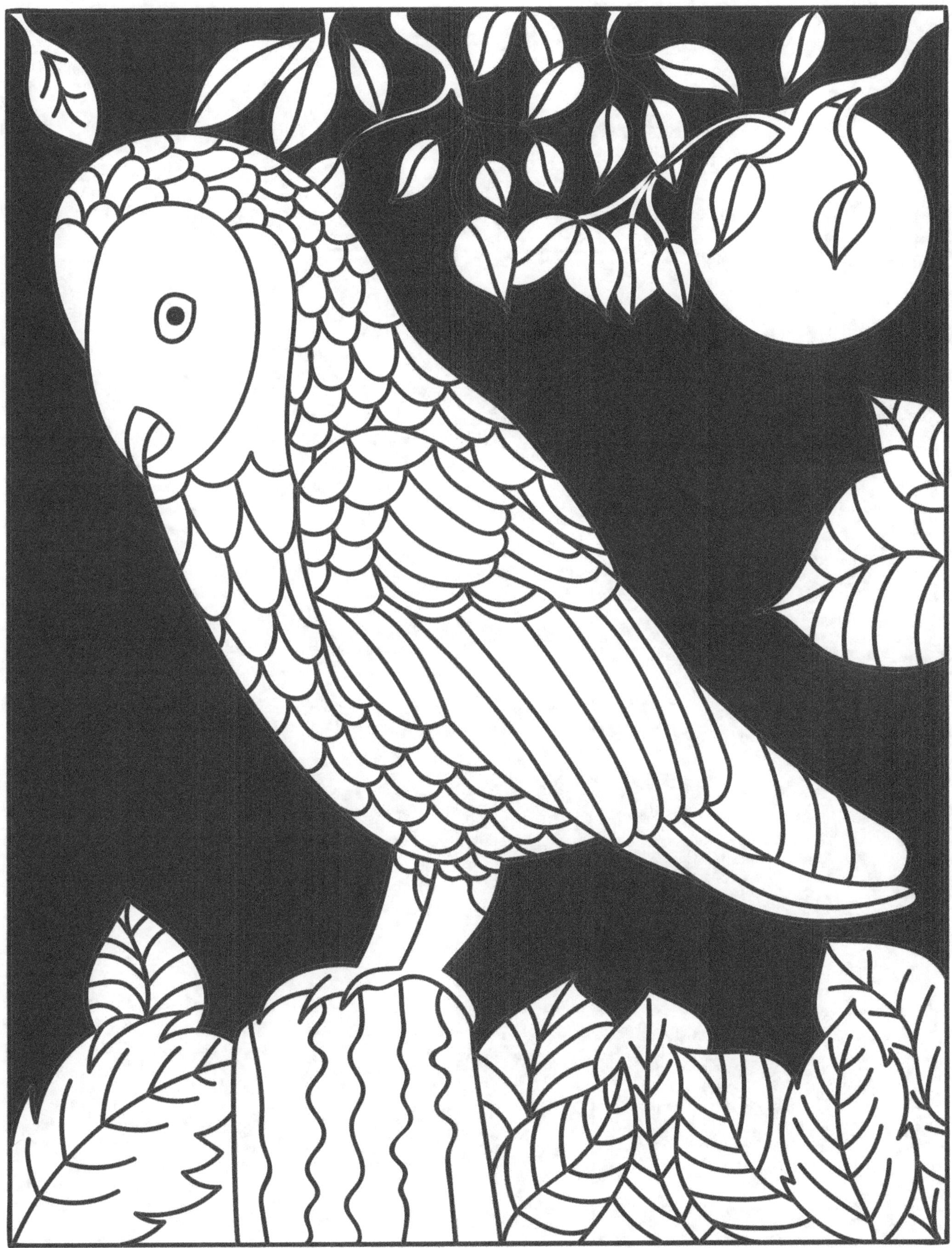

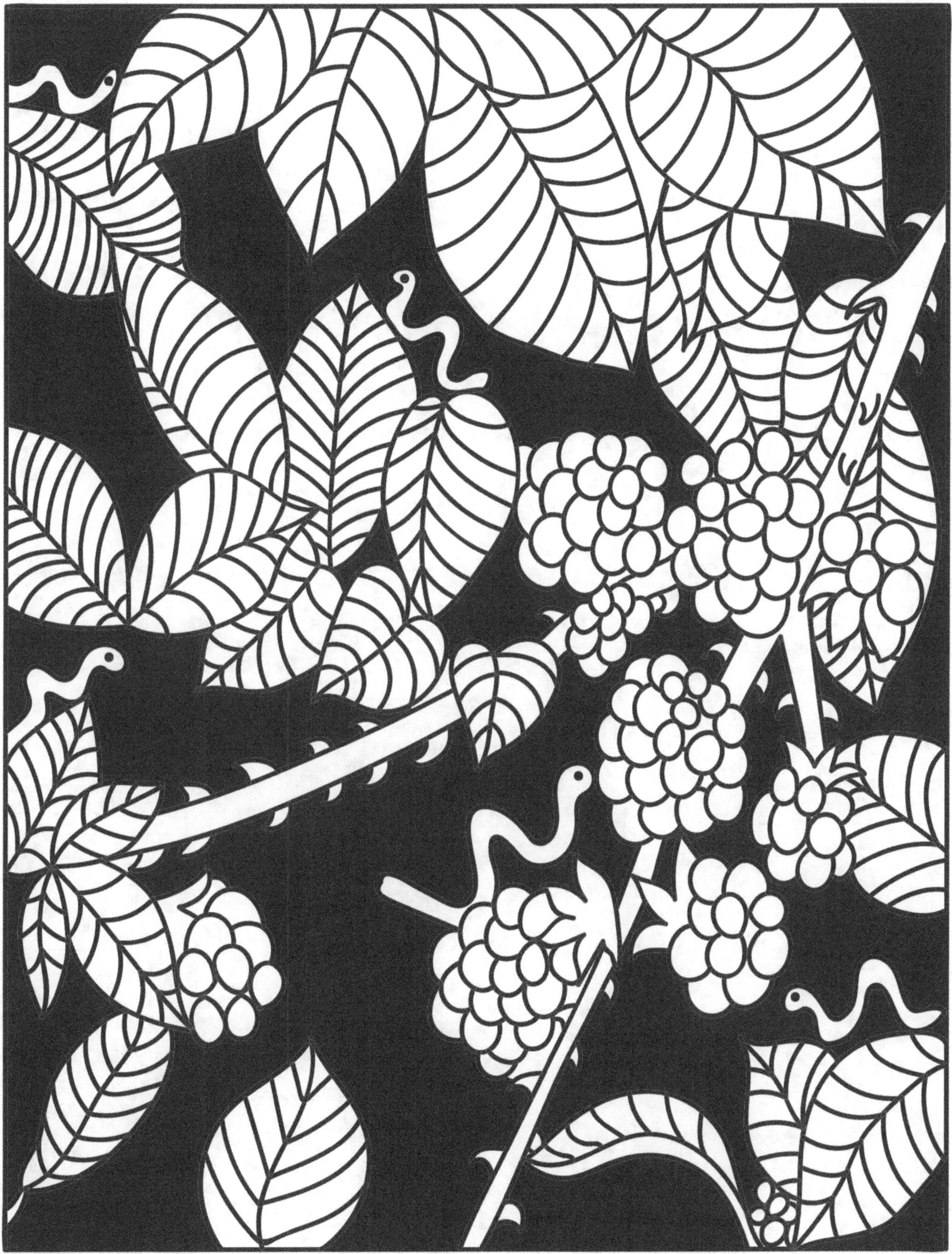

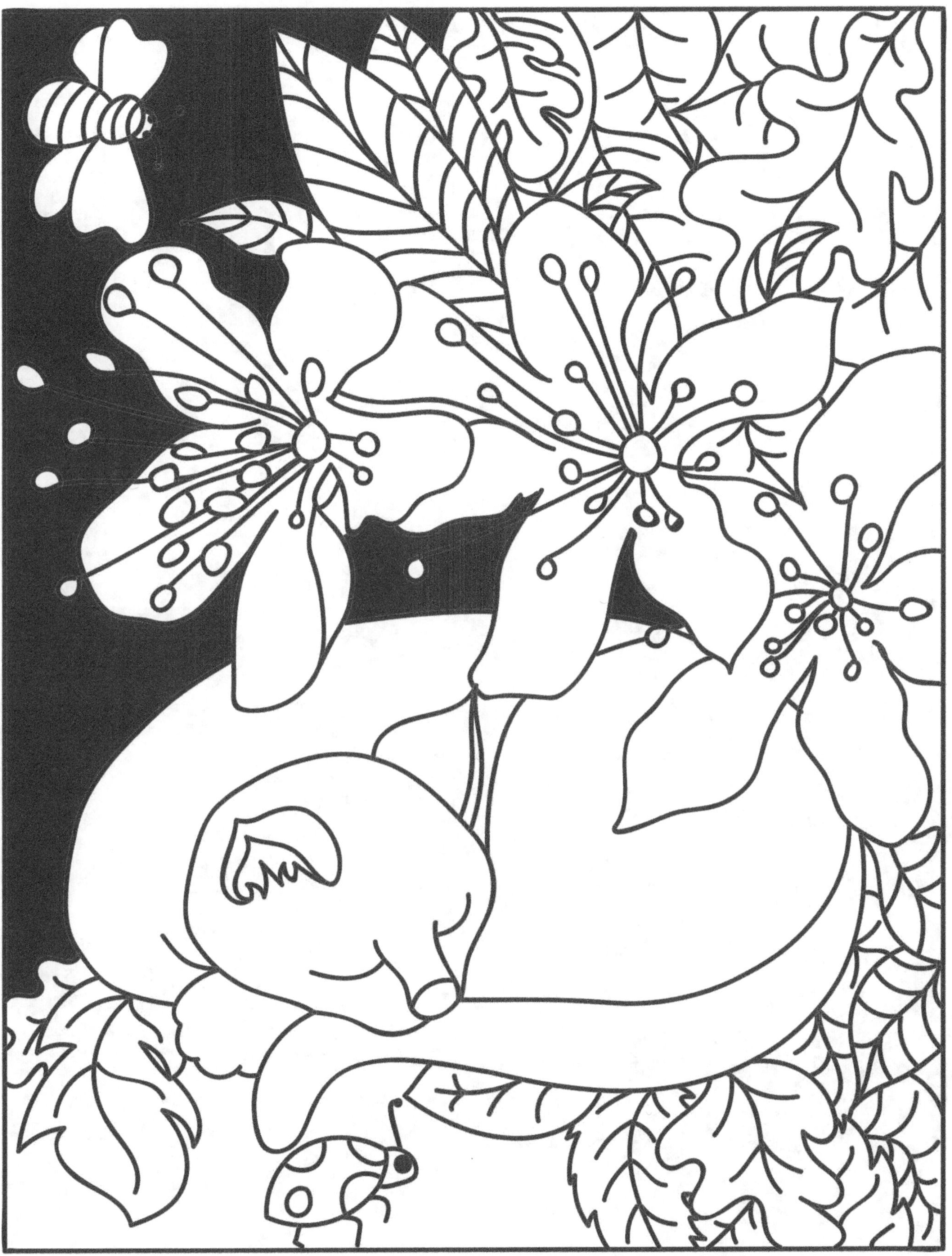

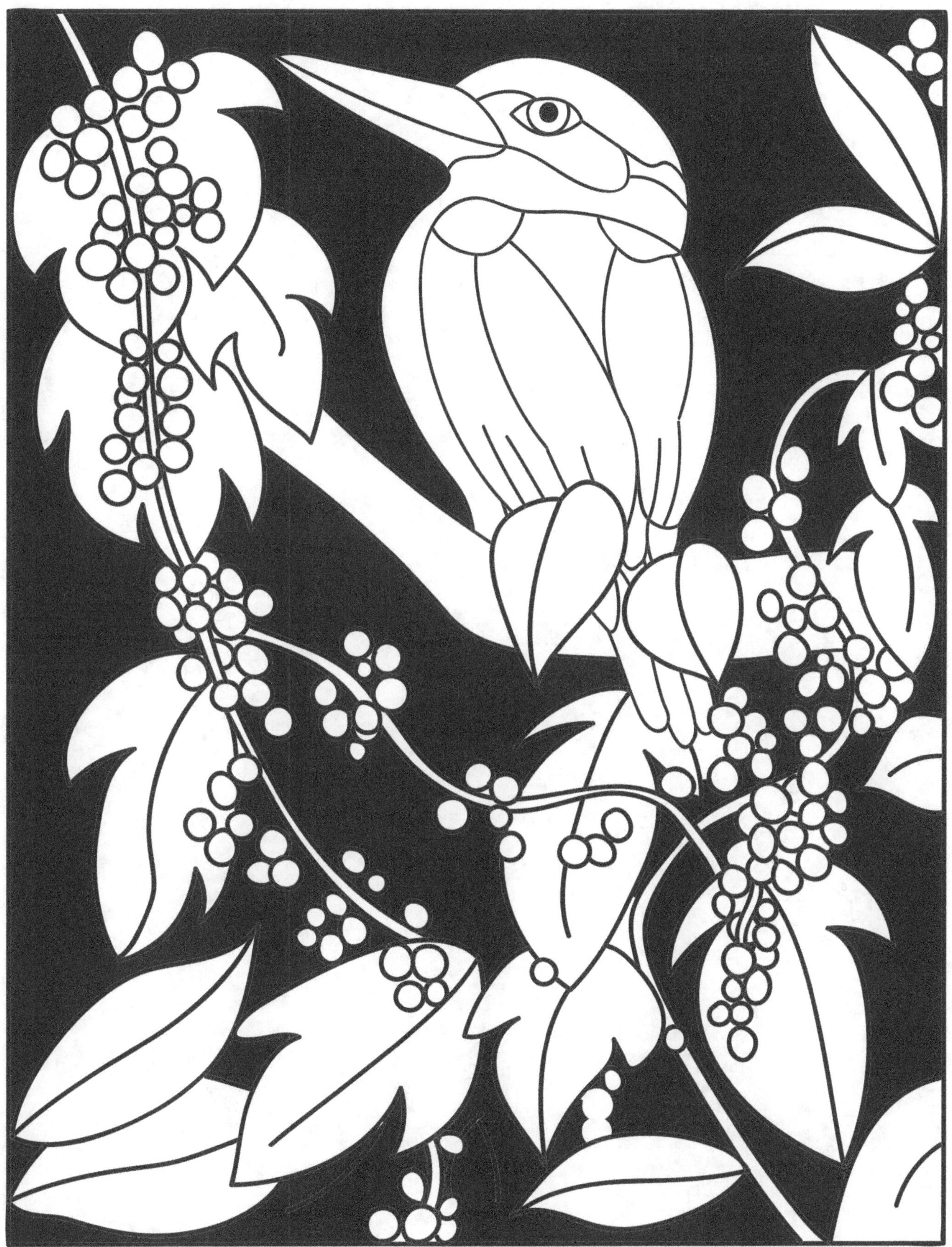

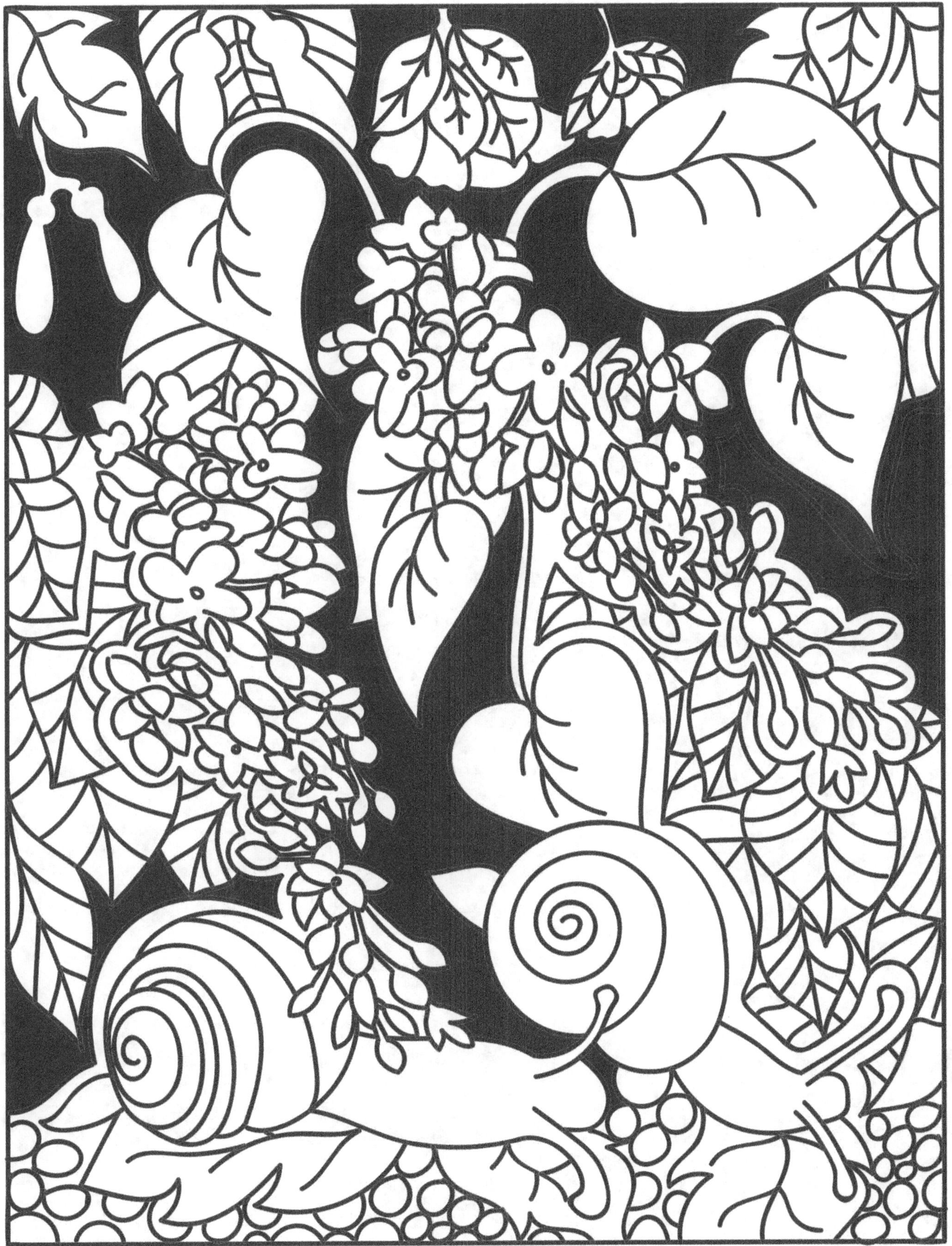

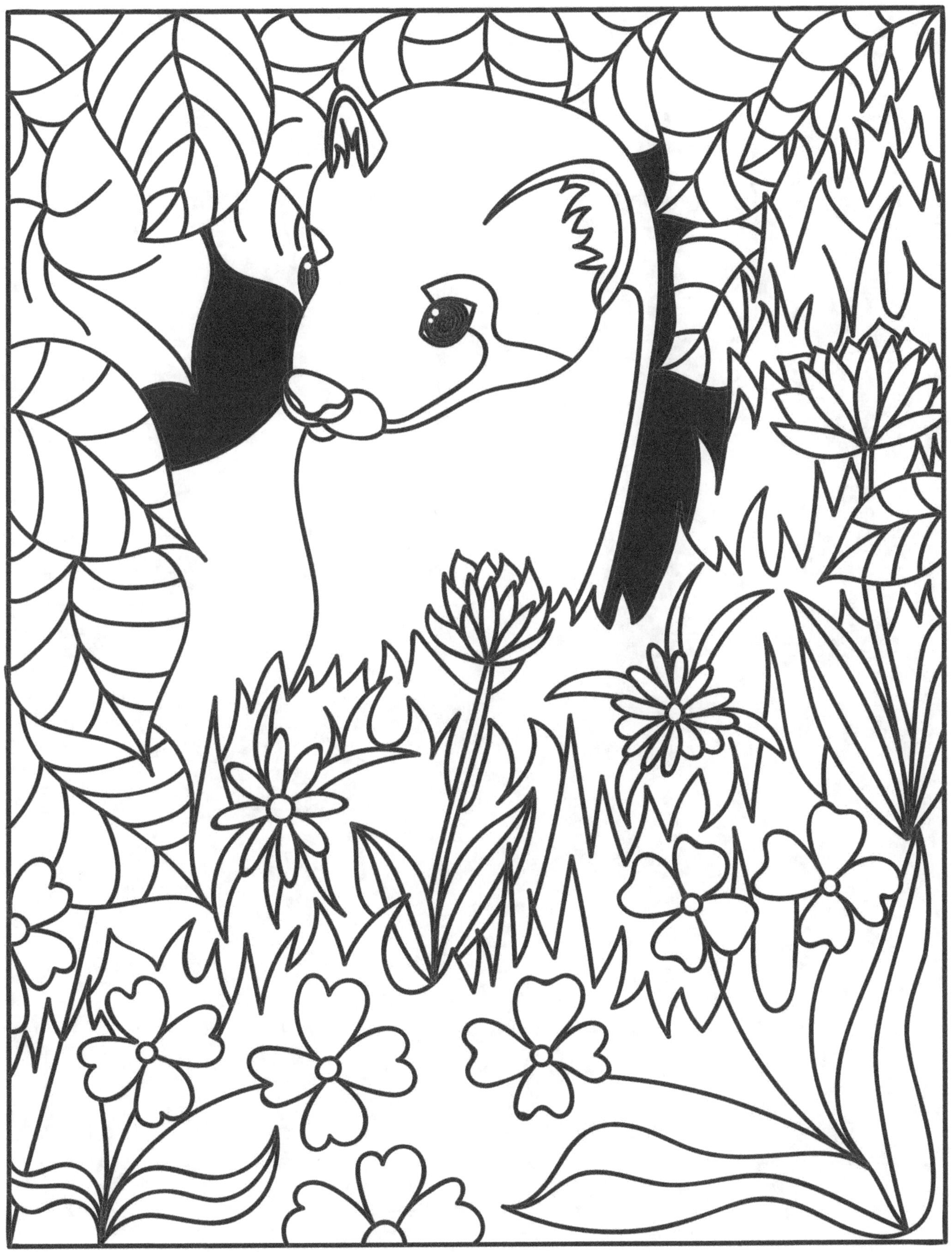

COLOR TEST PAGE

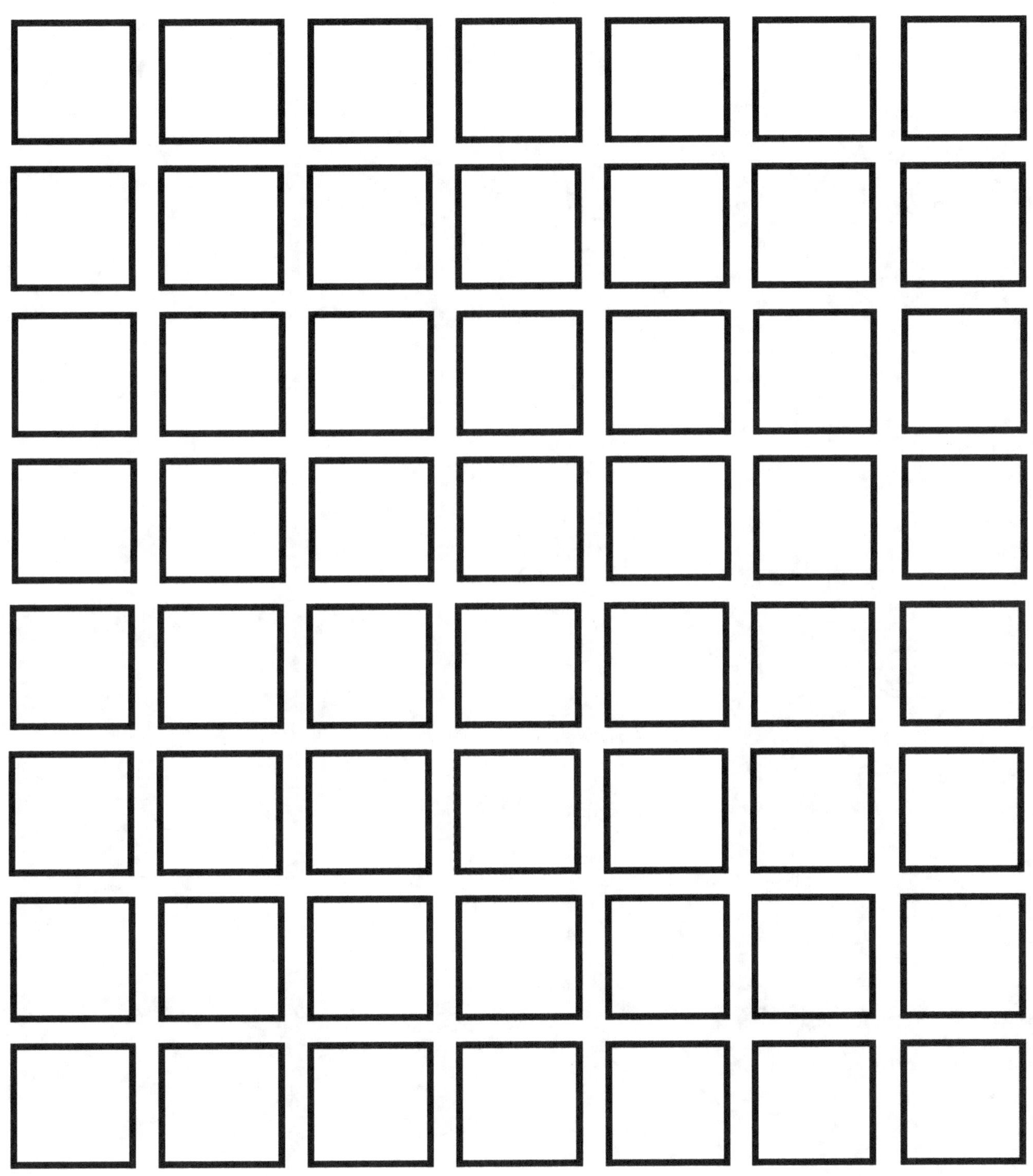

COLOR TEST PAGE

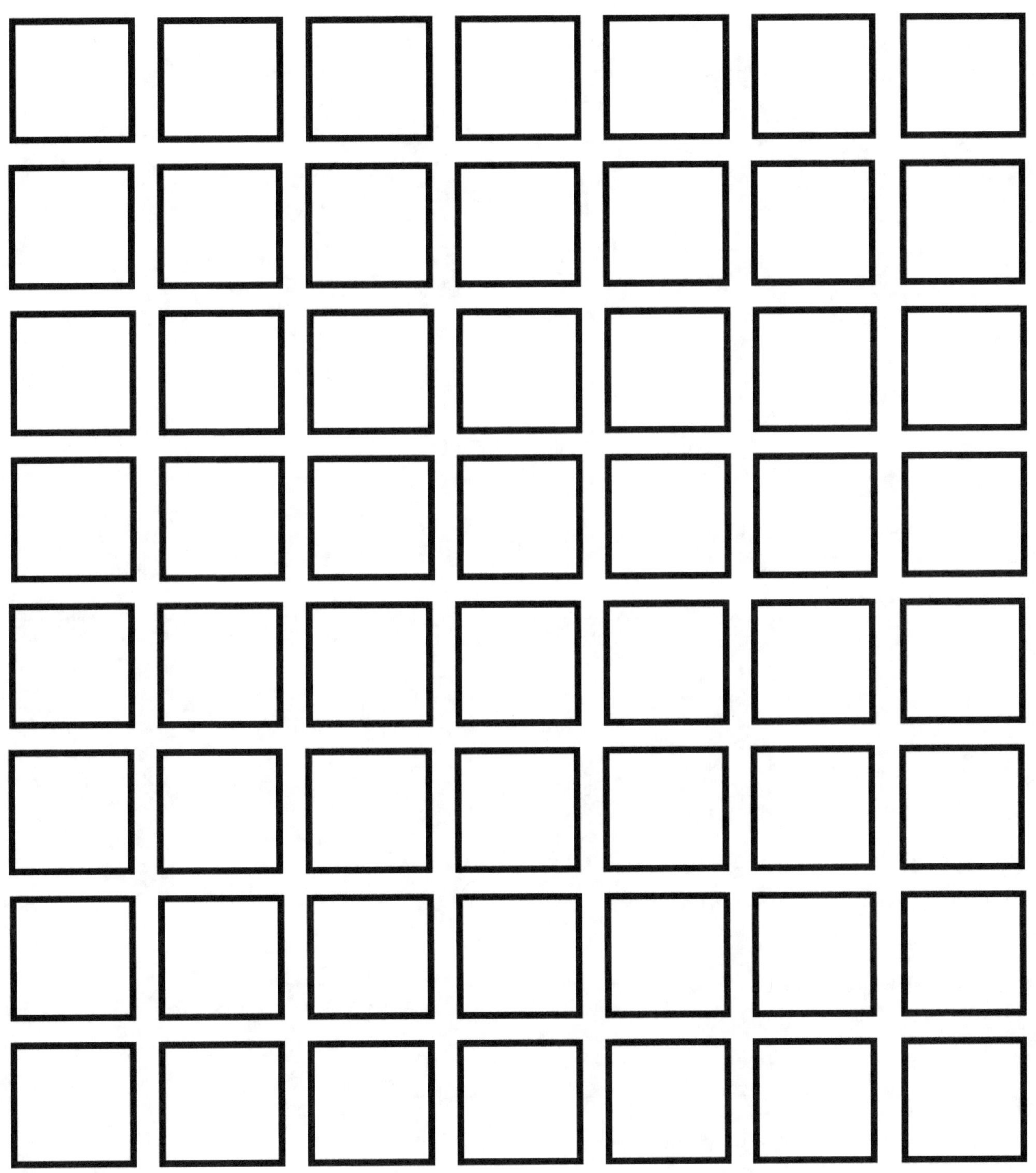